Other fun and informative products

from Tyndale House:

101 Fun Bible Word Searches

The Complete Book of Bible Trivia

Willmington's Book of Bible Lists

Humor Is Tremendous

The Book Game

People and Places in the Book Game

101 Fun BIBLE CROSSWORDS

Living Books®
Tyndale House Publishers, Inc.
Wheaton, Illinois

Living Books is a registered trademark
of Tyndale House Publishers, Inc.

ISBN 0-8423-0976-4
Printed in the United States of America

7   8   93   92

PUZZLES

ACROSS

1. Saul tried to kill him
6. Polite address used in the plural in Acts
10. Canaanite city that defeated Israel's first attack
11. Highest degree
12. Christians should do this to Satan
13. Word indicating a choice and used 1,015 times in the Authorized Version
14. According to a verse in Psalm 148, God's name is this
15. Baal of the Babylonians
18. Word indicating exclusion from and used 684 times in the Authorized Version
21. Jesus accused the Laodicean church of being this
24. Another term for death
26. There is only one
27. Town in Issachar
30. God's description of Phinehas
32. Jesus is the Prince of this
35. "_____, I am with you alway"
36. Valley on the border of Moab and Edom
38. From Issachar; judged Israel 23 years
39. City or district in Moab
40. Jesus told the Laodicean church to use this against spiritual blindness
41. Weak

DOWN

1. Priest in the time of Moses
2. Used to carry a body
3. Lysanias was tetrarch here
4. God views this as murder
5. The Tower of Babel was supposed to "_____ unto heaven"
6. Holding place for a horse
7. Name meaning "watcher"
8. This belongs to God
9. Jesus _____ the disciples to spread the gospel
16. Synonym for "humble"
17. 12th letter of the Greek alphabet
19. Jewish teacher
20. Direction indicating height; used 2,484 times in the Authorized Version
21. Unit of volume
22. Young goat
23. Restraining device on an animal's mouth
24. Action breaking the 8th Commandment
25. Judah's eldest son killed by God for his wickedness
28. Expresses prohibition and is used 1,377 times in the Authorized Version
29. Another name for Jacob
31. Moved into Sodom
32. Color of Death's horse in Revelation
33. Denotes a position; used 1,536 times in the Authorized Version
34. Famed priest and scribe

PUZZLE 1

DOWN

37. Denotes affirmative action; used 1,331 times in the Authorized Version
39. Denotes a comparison; used 3,369 times in the Authorized Version

ACROSS

1. Noah fell into this state
6. Enemy
8. Greek letter akin to Hebrew *resh*
10. Jesus is this
11. God is described in Psalms as our _____
14. Immeasurably long period of time
15. Chosen to replace Judas Iscariot
16. Fifth son of Jacob
18. Semitransparent pungent resin
21. Lethal surface of a sword
22. Second person singular
23. Abraham's nephew
25. Day celebrating Christ's resurrection
27. One name for a region where Christ healed a demoniac
30. In weakness we receive God's _____
35. Mountain on which the ark rested
36. Used in the plural to mean "news"

DOWN

1. Earth
2. Town of Zebulun
3. Consulting with the dead
4. God's see everything
5. James and John asked Jesus if they could do this at His sides
6. Symbol of eternal life
7. Measure of capacity
9. Frequently
12. Lucifer
13. State of wasteful inactivity
17. Sellers of goods
18. What blind Isaac did to Jacob
19. Eldest son of Caleb
20. In the plural, this is found in the sign God gave Noah
24. Definite article used 36,466 times in the Authorized Version
26. Opposite of wrong
28. Israelite judge who slew King Eglon
31. Another word for pitch
32. Peter cut one off
33. Jesus told the Laodicean church to be this or cold
34. King of Bashan

ACROSS

1. Brass washstand used in the tabernacle
4. Jew who rebelled against Rome
8. Proclaimed from experience
9. Twenty-second letter of the Greek alphabet
10. Nebuchadnezzar brought one against Jerusalem
11. Tools used to break ground
13. Son of Benjamin
15. She was a first
18. Sorrow
19. Used to catch fish
20. The Psalmist's reaction when invited to God's house
22. _____ of Life
23. Portable sanctuary
27. Israel's twin
28. Sign of God's covenant with Noah
30. Old name for Palestine
31. _____ to God!

DOWN

1. Thrown as a means of making a decision
2. Items used in the tabernacle
3. Lift up
4. Part of leg touched during an oath
5. Paul told Timothy to do this to afflictions
6. Luke was one
7. Old Testament secret agents
10. Power and might
12. Jesus' ministry to the sick
14. Masculine pronoun used 9,964 times in the Authorized Version
16. The _____ of time
17. Christ gave him a new name and a new life
21. Lasting forever
24. Vessel for washing
25. Substance used in making pottery
26. Used to call attention to
29. Jesus is the only _____ to salvation

PUZZLE 3

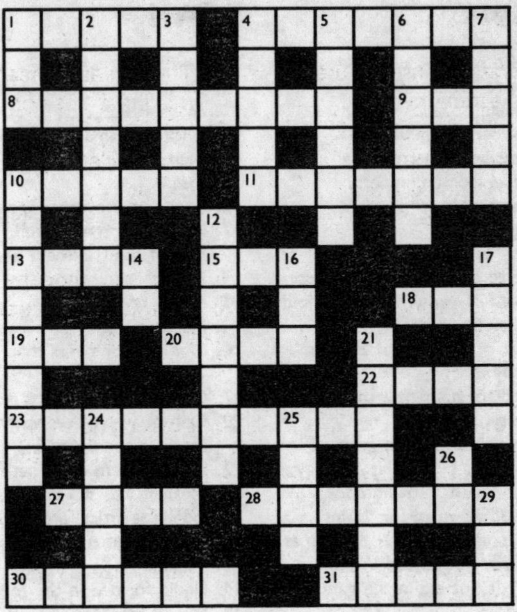

ACROSS

1. Price paid for a captive
4. God's Word tells us what we should _____
6. She served the church
8. City or district of Moab
9. Cruel Roman emperor responsible for Paul's execution
10. City of Judah
11. He received Manasseh's blessing
15. Form of gypsum used to hold precious ointments
18. Part of the king of Egypt's army
19. Soldiers guarding Jesus were guilty of this
20. Amphibian sent in great numbers by God against Egypt
21. Plant with a strong odor
22. Another word for "pains"
25. Preposition used 14,130 times in the Authorized Version
26. What Lot did in the gate of Sodom
27. Possess
28. Evangelist who baptized the Ethiopian eunuch
30. Son of Aram
31. At Christ's return, the Christian will be changed in one of these
33. Brother of Abel
35. Satan comes to do this
36. Should be done to one's own actions before others'

DOWN

1. Run this to win
2. Drink offered Jesus on the cross was _____
3. Another name for the wise men
5. Last
6. Loose or irreverent speech
7. Christ sees the Church as this
12. Ark of the Covenant kept in here
13. Father of Anak
14. Material wealth or possessions
16. One of four rivers that watered Eden
17. Jesus encountered this
20. One of two places where the mark of the Beast will go
22. Modern form of "pineth" meaning "to sicken"
23. Indefinite article used 1,660 times in the Authorized Version
24. Liquid formed in the mouth
28. Son of Issachar
29. Father of Shuppim and Huppim
32. Number of sisters Lazarus had
34. No vacancy here for Joseph and Mary

ACROSS

1. Name of the gate at the temple where a lame man was healed
6. Balaam rode this
8. Symbol of strength, _____ of God
9. Another name for Tadmor
11. The result of weeping
12. Class distinction of soldiers
14. Father of Eliel
16. God promised Abraham he would be a father of many _____
19. Hot oven in which Daniel's friends were placed
20. She was not immune to temptation
21. Large group of soldiers
23. To gather together
25. Paul knew it well
26. To decorate

DOWN

1. John the _____
2. Jesus wants the Christian to surrender _____
3. Attempt
4. One of the gifts for Baby Jesus
5. Jesus is the first and _____
6. Father of Moses
7. God created four of these
10. Another gift brought by the wise men
13. Jesus was born in here
17. Admired for its beauty in the Middle East
18. Two-word name God told Moses to call Him
19. _____ of Tabernacles
22. Affirmative; used only 4 times in the Authorized Version
24. Another word for "insane"

PUZZLE 5

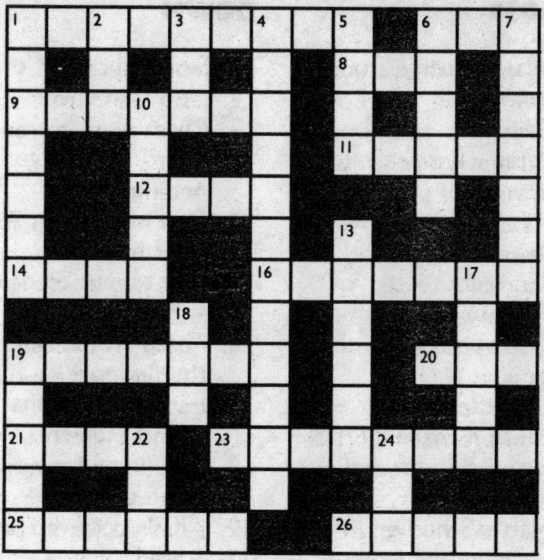

ACROSS

1. Was formerly a tax collector
5. Gain
9. Peter went there to pray
10. Solomon was wiser than he
11. Fourteenth letter of Hebrew alphabet
13. God's reaches to the clouds
17. Gird these
18. Bread is made of this
20. Jesus often made a _____ to Mary and Martha's home
21. He returned from captivity
23. Hateful or nasty
25. Built
27. Keeper of David's camels
28. "_____ ye doers of the word"
29. Number of times Jesus died for our sins
30. Joseph was put in one of these by Potiphar

DOWN

1. Second book in the New Testament
2. Pair
3. Word used to get one's attention
4. One involved in the black arts
6. Paul tells us to do this well
7. Three words naming the first writing instrument of the Ten Commandments
8. Paul knew how to make these
12. Judas's betrayed Jesus
13. Scared
14. Where Christ should rank in your life
15. Moses did this with the rod of God
16. To speak falsely against another
19. Another name for the Egyptian god, Ra
22. Associated with a poor widow
23. Israelites complained that they didn't have this food
24. Planter of seed used in a parable

DOWN

27. Form the Holy Spirit used when appearing at Jesus' baptism

ACROSS

1. Disease of the skin
5. Fifteenth letter of Hebrew alphabet
8. Symbol used by early Christians
9. Uncontrolled mob action
10. Onan's older brother
11. Paralytic healed through Peter's prayer
13. Provided the lunch Jesus used to feed 5,000
14. We are created in God's _____
15. Murdered by his brother
16. Judas took care of this, but dishonestly
19. Another word for "spirit"
20. To put trust in
21. Nature of God
23. Bird of the night
24. Oldest daughter of Agrippa I
25. To charge with a crime
27. Proverbs tells us to be _____ to anger
29. Power associated with God

DOWN

1. Name for God
2. Describes an extravagant son in the New Testament
3. Feminine pronoun used 1,022 times in the Authorized Version
4. Type of herb
5. Three words describing a famous valley
6. Miracle food given to the Israelites
7. Ancient people
12. Quietness
17. Varieties of this used in cooking and medicine
18. Language in which most of the Old Testament was written
19. Kernels of corn and wheat
20. Relative
22. Called "Abib" in the Pentateuch
26. "I _____ do all things through Christ"
27. Member of David's mighty men
28. Having to do with prolonged age

ACROSS

33. Eternal life is the Christian's _____
36. Anointed the first two kings of Israel
37. Jacob made one from a stone

DOWN

30. Solid water; only mentioned 3 times in the Authorized Version
31. Misguided target of worship
32. Christians are to _____ spiritually
34. Hebrew word meaning "God"
35. Title of 17th division of Psalm 119

ACROSS

1. Cultivation tool
5. Roman centurion
7. Used to remove ashes
8. Remains from a fire
9. Name for Satan
11. Precious stone
12. Suitor's offering for a bride
13. Solomon's ships brought this animal to Israel
15. Valley where Achan and his family were stoned
17. Joseph's brothers cast him in one
18. Dry measure of about 1 quart
20. What others think of you
23. "_____ saith the Lord"
24. Not tainted with sin

DOWN

2. Son of Bani
3. Town ascribed to Benjamin
4. Wise king
5. Province in Palestine
6. On the floor of the desert
7. Tabernacle holy bread
10. Latin salute
14. Friend and fellow minister with Paul
16. Eleventh letter of the Hebrew alphabet
18. Measure equal to about 10 1/2 bushels
19. Jesus is the _____ of Life
21. Righteous king of Judah
22. Sixteenth letter in the Greek alphabet

PUZZLE 8

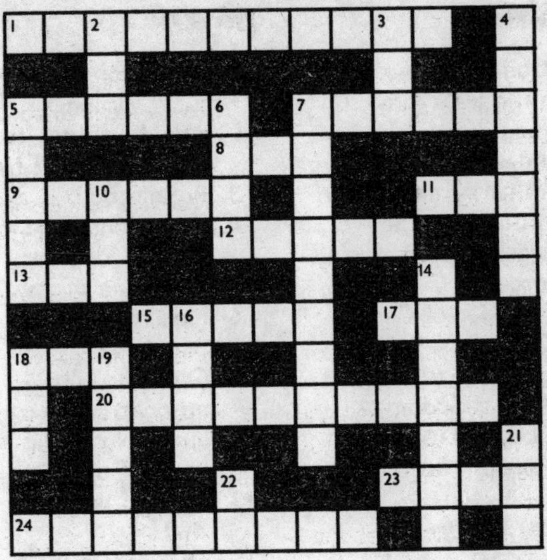

ACROSS

1. Godly tolerance
7. Who Jesus came to redeem
8. Adversary
9. What Adam and Eve brought on the world
11. Israelites crossed _____ Jordan
12. Follower of Christ
14. One of Esau's wives
17. Used to crush grapes
21. King of Sodom
23. Birthplace of Nahum
24. Absalom fled on one

DOWN

1. Revelation describes a _____ prophet
2. Asked Deborah to ride into battle with him
3. Boring tool
4. Fifth month of the Hebrew calendar
5. Top stone of a wall
6. Modern word for "mustereth"
9. One who is held prisoner
10. In the plural, this is a book of the Bible
13. Used to tie down or bind
15. The man at the Gate Beautiful was _____
16. Jesus sent some demons into them
18. A millstone sometimes hung here
19. Ancestress of King David
20. Jesus' garment didn't have one
21. Eighth Jewish month
22. Jesus did this for the disciples to prove He was no ghost

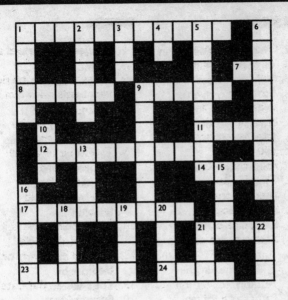

ACROSS

2. Third foundation stone of the Holy City
7. Held up Moses' hand
8. Paul was converted near there
12. David's grandfather
13. Like a well
14. Side
16. Sixth king of Israel
17. One who tells falsehoods
18. Evil spirit
19. Destructive insect
21. God supplies every one
23. Antonym of "in"; used 2,696 times in the Authorized Version
24. Father of Eliasaph
25. Deeper parts of a river
26. Seaport of Lycia
27. Esau could do this well
28. Shaking of the earth

DOWN

1. Government official
3. Home of the stars
4. To gain knowledge
5. To plaster
6. Tenth letter of the Hebrew alphabet
9. "Being _____ of this very thing"
10. Land in Ethiopia
11. Goddess of the Assyrians and Babylonians
15. Early Christian theological term relating to the Incarnation
19. Lot's sister
20. Stinging insect
22. Elijah's successor
24. Mephibosheth was this

PUZZLE 10

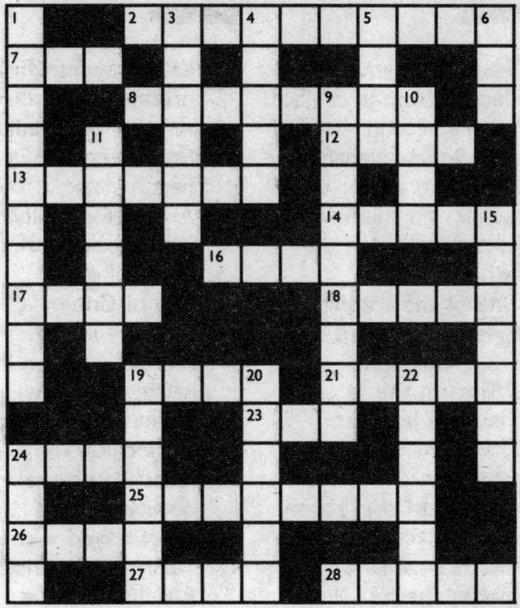

ACROSS

1. Tender concern
3. Plucked from Jesus' face
8. Twenty-second letter of the Hebrew alphabet
9. Protective barrier used against the enemy
10. Jesus called Satan the father of one
12. One of the apostles
15. Hide God's Word _____ our heart
16. Will form the gates of the New Jerusalem
18. Tender mercy and caring
21. He joined David's army
22. Worship festival
24. Another name for Shelah, Shem's grandson
26. Thick thread
27. Number of unfaithful spies
28. Overflowing

DOWN

1. Letter written from prison
2. A weed of grainfields
3. Esther was known for hers
4. Animal exemplifying a hard worker
5. Sense of guilt
6. Son of Coz
7. Helem was his father
11. Famous question in Isaiah, "_____ will go?"
12. Went with Paul to Antioch
13. Judas did not have this quality
14. Elijah stayed with one
17. Denotes existence; used 845 times in the Authorized Version
19. Measure equalling about 3 1/2 quarts
20. Holy
23. _____ on the Lord
25. Old _____, a reward for obedience

PUZZLE 11

ACROSS

1. Ephron was one
5. Offered a pleasing sacrifice to God
7. Means "fool"
9. City where the church was lukewarm
10. Third son of Shela; his uncle had the same name
11. Og's was made of iron
16. Ezekiel used this name when prophesying against Jerusalem
18. We are this when we accept Christ
23. To submit
24. A grandson of Benjamin
25. Authorized Version calls it "anise"
26. Esau's first wife
30. Border of a garment
32. Two words; one part of the house painted with lamb's blood
34. God's endures forever
35. Noah sent one from the ark
36. Wise men came from there

DOWN

1. Moses received a challenge here
2. God will take these away
3. Place where food sits
4. Decaying inner wood gives off a fragrant resin
5. Son of Rehoboam
6. Egyptians sank like this in the Red Sea
8. Used 3,002 times in the Authorized Version; sounds like a letter
12. Can also be translated "wearing sandals"
13. "Thy will be _____"
14. Accuse
15. Made in God's image
17. Mixed, like fire and hail
18. One of Esau's Hittite wives
19. To be sick
20. Colored artificially
21. There was a tower here
22. This should never be done to God's Word
27. Jesus, name _____ all names
28. Gopher or ebony

DOWN

29. Jesus said Christians are this
31. "_____ hath not seen"
33. Definite article, used 36,466 times in the Authorized Version

ACROSS

1. Struggle or dissension
6. Citadel near Jerusalem
7. Various grasses bearing edible seeds
9. Joseph's father-in-law was a priest here
10. "I am the _____, the truth, and the life"
11. This grows on a tree and is pressed for oil
14. An unhealthy characteristic
16. Teams with the Antichrist; two words
18. Paul appeared before him
19. Ancestor of Christ
21. Humble in spirit
24. Separates us from God
25. Jesus is the same _____, today, and forever
26. She was a widow of 84 years when she first saw Jesus

DOWN

1. Pack animal well suited to desert travel
2. Togetherness
3. Philistine in the army of David
4. What the archers did to King Saul
5. Can mean "separated to God"
8. Tool used for cultivating
10. Type of bread used in the temple
12. Goodness
13. A small amount: Bit
15. _____ the cross
17. Tool used to chop wood
18. Outrage
20. Tasted like wafers with honey
21. Muck
22. Father of the Edomites
23. Maachah was his evil grandmother
24. Created on the fourth day

PUZZLE 13

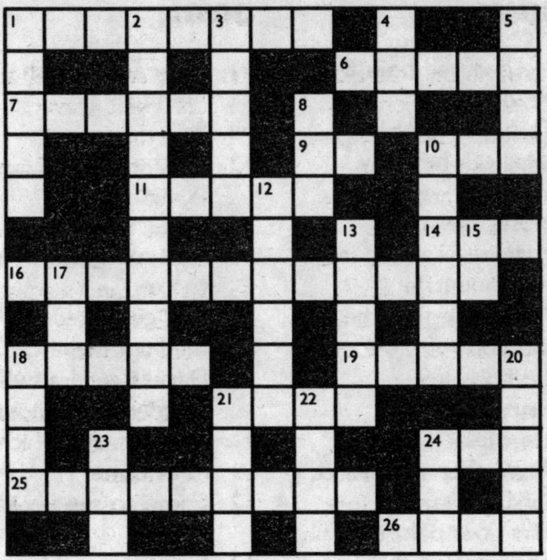

ACROSS

1. He endured boils from head to toe
3. To gather crops
8. Jesus can heal any variety
9. Moses saw the Promised Land from this mountain
10. "_____ ye first the kingdom of God"
12. "Who is my _____?"
15. Jesus is the Vine, we are these
18. Town that was spared for Lot's sake
19. This goes before a fall
20. They denied the resurrection of the dead
23. David laid the Moabites out in three of these
25. Together; only used once in the Authorized Version
26. God always does this for our needs

DOWN

1. Later form of the name "Joshua"
2. Pail
3. "Is the Lord's _____ waxed short?"
4. _____ of Sharon
5. God met with Moses there
6. Saul consulted a medium there
7. David's general who murdered Absalom
11. Nation from which Ruth came
12. Came to see Jesus by night
13. Good news
14. Brother of Buz
15. Old manna _____ worms
16. Ring or a seal
17. Disciples were mending these when Jesus came
21. From a distance
22. One of David's Levite musicians
24. Joshua's father

ACROSS

2. Jesus was brought up here
5. Jesse's father
8. Book before Nehemiah
9. Only right reply to temptation
10. Satan's activity
11. Another name for Jerusalem
12. Affirmative, trustworthy
14. Malchus lost one but Jesus healed it
15. Descendants of Shem
17. Ingredient in John the Baptist's diet
19. Name meaning "of the ground"
21. Oversaw the Nethinims
23. Bartimaeus could _____ after Jesus healed him
25. Our go-between
27. "_____ is finished"
28. "Offend in one point . . . guilty of _____"
29. Husband of Sapphira; tried to deceive God
31. "Thou shalt have no other gods before _____"

DOWN

1. Non-Jews
2. Weakest point in a city's walls
3. Fixture in the tabernacle
4. Old spelling of "loathe"
5. Town about six miles southeast of Joppa
6. Ezekiel saw a valley of these
7. Blood was painted around this at the Passover
11. Joram conquered the Edomites here
13. Laban was Jacob's _____
16. Died at the news of his sons' deaths
18. Deceived Judah
20. Digging tool
21. Twentieth of a shekel
22. Ancestor of Maaseiah, a Jewish prince
24. Garden home
25. Means "What is it?"
26. Soldiers from this town killed about 36 Israelites
29. He shall gather the lambs with his _____

34

ACROSS

32. Land measurement
33. Helped conduct a Levitical prayer in Nehemiah's day

DOWN

30. Satan is "the prince of the power of the _____"

ACROSS

1. Eliphaz's concubine
4. Another name for Ben-Ammi
8. Another name for a cast lot
9. Job sat in this
10. Where Cain dwelt after killing Abel
11. Another name for Azariah, Daniel's friend
13. Jacob changed the name to Bethel
15. "Their _____ dieth not"; describes hell
16. Testament containing 39 books
17. Greek form of the name "Neriah"
20. _____ the Hararite
23. Master shipbuilder
25. To set apart
26. "_____ saith the Lord"
27. To die
28. "_____ to laugh"
29. Scroll
30. How quickly James and John left fishing to follow Jesus

DOWN

1. Sound of small bells
2. Elisha told King Joash to shoot one
3. Joshua was one when he first visited Canaan
4. City given to Judah
5. Small Galilean town also called Dalmanutha
6. "Blessed be the _____ of the Lord"
7. His brother, Uzzah, died for touching the Ark
11. Minor prophet
12. Two words describing Israel's idol at Sinai
14. Fenced city of Naphtali
18. "_____ thine ear unto wisdom"
19. In the beginning it was void
21. Means "messenger" or "ambassador"
22. One who gathers
24. Used in making bread
27. Next to the last letter in the Greek alphabet

ACROSS

1. Describes human nature
4. This will signal Christ's return
9. People chosen by God to foretell events
10. David hid in one
11. Mountain marking one of the boundaries of Joshua's conquests
13. Expression of dismay or sorrow
16. She asked for John the Baptist's head
19. To break a marriage
20. Saul's former general who tried to make peace with David
21. Before God, nations are "as a _____ of a bucket"
23. To submit to God
25. Divided the holy place from the holy of holies
27. Jacob was one
28. We should _____ our wills to God
29. Mound of waste

DOWN

2. Reverence and praise to God
3. To make right or change for the better
5. To scoff
6. Soldiers did this to Jesus
7. Number of disciples
8. Tree
9. Jesus taught us how to do this
12. King of Judah whose name means "physician"
14. Made some soup poisonous
15. Can mean "reverence"
16. Paul saw one go to pieces
17. Rachel's older sister
18. "Oh that _____ would praise the Lord"
20. Jesus experienced this for us
21. He wrote and sang many songs
22. Used to grind grain
24. Was formed from a rib
26. Moses and his family stayed in one
27. King of Hamath whose name means "wanderer"

PUZZLE 17

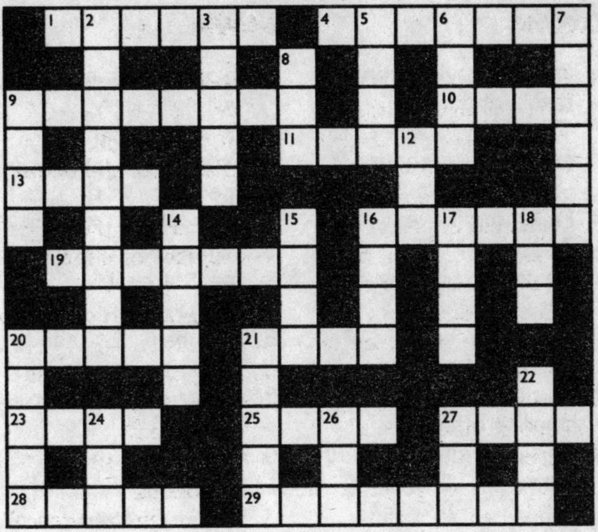

ACROSS

1. Revelation gives some details about this
7. "The glory of the Lord _____ round about them"
8. Philemon's slave
11. To jump
13. Hatred or hostility
16. Puteoli was one
17. Terah died here
21. Philistine champion
22. Burned as a sweet-smelling offering
23. Sign or symbol of good faith

DOWN

2. Type of person who will go hungry
3. Goliath's brother
4. Possessive pronoun only used once in the Authorized Version
5. Haman had one ready for Mordecai
6. Job had 7,000
8. Jesus died _____ and for all
9. Father of one of Moses' 12 spies
10. God's gift of grace
11. Jesus is the _____ of God
12. Levite city in Manasseh
14. Synonym for clemency
15. Metal
17. Gad's son
18. Spring in Jerusalem
19. Peter _____ when he took his eyes off Jesus
20. Jacob prophesied that he would be like a serpent

ACROSS

1. One who consults the stars
7. Midianite king killed by the Israelites
9. Represented a small sin
10. Benjamite
11. Isaiah used it to describe the remnant of Israel
12. Jesus did this on the ground when healing a blind man
13. Where the story of Jesus is found
16. Brought about the destruction of a wicked human race
18. Solomon imported this from Egypt
20. To do wrong
22. Egyptian city called "Heliopolis" by the Greeks
24. God gives every good and perfect one
25. Most important one is to receive Christ
26. Disciples found a donkey _____ with a colt

DOWN

2. Ahasuarus had one of gold
3. Kingdom
4. Were chosen to be priests and temple workers
5. Rebellious Israelites this age and older never saw the Promised Land
6. "_____ ye into all the world, and preach the gospel"
8. Sister of Aaron and Moses
9. A truth only known by revelation
13. Mighty hunter
14. Torment, anxiety, distress
15. Moses' mother sealed his basket with this
17. City in Judah
19. Famous
21. Pharaoh gave Joseph his
23. Used to gather fish
24. "_____ thee behind me, Satan"

ACROSS

1. Christ has given us _____ from sin
7. A people east of the Tigris who were about to invade Judah
8. "In the _____"
10. Feeling remorse
11. Used in the worship of God
12. Restrained and guided oxen
14. "Thy _____ come"
18. One of Esau's father-in-laws
19. Vessel holding the tabernacle's water
20. Sandal
21. Edge of a container
22. Achan hid stolen booty under his
24. Put through a servant's ear
26. Revelation describes one with seven heads
27. Israel crossed the Jordan on _____ ground
28. Insect that helped inspire Samson's riddle
29. God provided this for Jonah

DOWN

2. First stone in the third row of a priest's breastplate
3. Ahab murdered Naboth for his
4. Dried grape
5. One of the five chief Philistine cities
6. In the baker's dream, he had three on his head
9. Lizard
10. Worn as a sign of mourning or sorrow
13. Relative
15. "_____ are thy tender mercies"
16. To ponder
17. Peleg's father
23. Solomon built one in Ezion-Geber
25. Title for Jesus Christ

ACROSS

1. Where Jesus performed his first public miracle
8. Language Jesus spoke
9. Jesus _____ for our sins
10. Title applied to Jesus
12. Very hard stone
14. His son hit Jeremiah
16. Nebuchadnezzar saw feet of _____ and clay
17. A flask or bottle
20. To give understanding
25. God told Israel to _____ their ways
26. Christian women are _____ in Christ
27. One of four on the high priest's breastplate

DOWN

2. Priest who returned from Babylon to Jerusalem
3. Crown
4. Samson was imprisoned there
5. Paul's teacher
6. Keep safe
7. English name for the ancient city of Accho
9. Legalistic religious leaders who opposed Jesus
10. God threatened to destroy this city
11. Another name for Noah
13. Powerful teacher in the early church
15. "Mercy and truth are _____ together"
18. Amazement or admiration
19. This moved backwards for King Hezekiah
21. Jesus "_____, and waxed strong in spirit"
22. Isaiah prophesied that God would _____ Shebna "like a ball"
23. In the same passage, God compares Eliakim to a _____
24. David killed one

PUZZLE 21

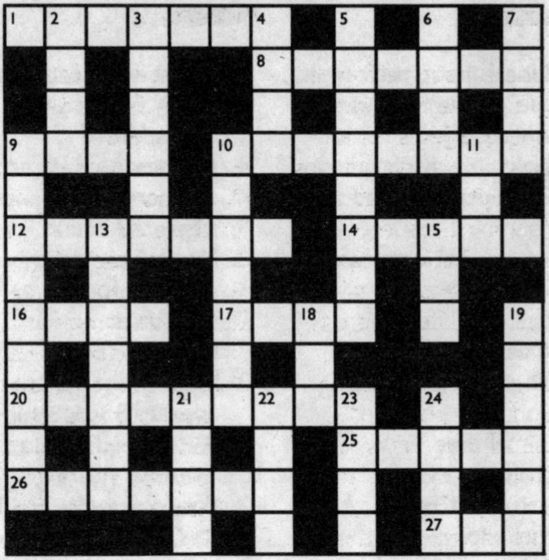

ACROSS

1. Musical instrument
3. One of the nails used on Jesus
7. Looks like an "x"
8. Can represent God's anger
11. "_____ there no balm in Gilead?"
12. _____ of Life
14. Queen of _____
15. We can call God _____
16. Sun god
19. Animal used as a sacrifice
20. Instrument of crucifixion
22. Also the sun god
23. Wartime tactic of surprise
26. Wafer
27. Bore the sins of Israel before Christ came
28. Each man in Judas's mob carried one

DOWN

2. Another word for tent peg
3. God's Word
4. Condition of Peter's mother-in-law
5. Repeated sound
6. Figuratively describes teaching for young Christians
8. Increases faith
9. Employ the function of; appears 35 times in the Authorized Version
10. Without hearing
12. Poor person's sacrifice to God
13. Used to move a boat
17. Old name was "Hai"
18. Place of sacrifice
19. Means "Anointed One"
21. "Widow and _____"
24. God spoke to Moses from a burning _____
25. To anticipate
26. Swaddling clothes and the manger were a _____ to the shepherds

PUZZLE 22

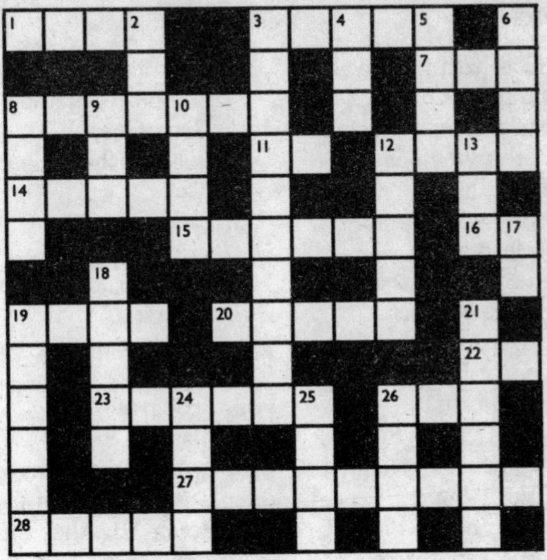

ACROSS

1. "God hath not given us the spirit of _____"
4. David compared himself to this when Saul chased him
6. Promised curse for disobedience
9. Jesus warned that this expression was dangerous
11. Land of Esau's descendants
13. "_____, though I walk through the valley"
14. "Take thine _____, eat, drink, and be merry"
15. Can mean "to test"
16. Rahab let the spies down with one
17. Portion owed to God
19. David's nephew slew a giant who had 12 of these
22. Arrested Christians before coming to Christ
23. An expression of surprise or joy
25. To kill
26. Was not to touch Samson

DOWN

1. Describes the two demoniacs of the Gergesenes
2. Built by the tribe of Gad
3. "Jealousy is the _____ of a man"
4. Pilate could find none in Jesus
5. Joseph rose to great power here
7. Prohibited body marking
8. Isaiah heard a heavenly being say this of God
10. Bound together the high priest's breastplate and ephod
12. Can mean "created"
18. Another word for "islands"
20. Celestial beings Isaiah described
21. Not restless
22. "I go to prepare a _____ for you"
24. Designates skill, craft, and cunning
25. Heard God's voice in his bedroom
27. Haman's wife

PUZZLE 23

ACROSS

28. "Ye are the _____ of the earth"
30. Absalom's mother
33. Snare
34. Kore's father
36. Sold his birthright for some soup
37. God knows the _____ from the beginning
38. One of Nebuchadnezzar's officials

DOWN

29. David chided him for sleeping on guard duty
31. Another word for "fever"
32. Sound of disapproval
35. "Hills once cultivated by the _____"

ACROSS

1. Tool used for carving
4. Kettle
7. God said he would _____ 15 years to Hezekiah's life
9. "Let us make man . . . after our _____"
10. God told the Israelites to _____ outside of Jericho
13. Light at night
14. God asked Jesus to _____ at his right hand
15. "He that hath an _____, let him hear"
16. We can't just hear God's Word; we must _____ what it says
17. Restored to health
19. Ruth's mother-in-law
22. Used to bake breads
23. Home of the grape
24. Female offspring
27. Plant used to sprinkle blood during Passover rites
29. Village of Galilee
31. Something held against someone
32. A particular historical period
34. Work
35. Corruption or sinfulness
37. There is only _____ God
38. To produce
40. "_____ ye doers of the Word"
42. Samson killed a big one
43. Produced by the olive
45. God sent this bird to feed Elijah
46. "I am the resurrection, and the _____"

DOWN

2. Try to keep from doing this spiritually
3. Achan's sin gave this city a victory
4. Convinced
5. Greek name for this city means "City of the Sun"
6. Natural part of life
7. Remains of burnt offerings
8. John the Baptist said he must do this
9. Promised _____
11. Forbidden food
12. "Ashes _____ ashes, dust _____ dust"
17. Pharaoh did this to his heart
18. We return to this
20. Spiritual world is this
21. Describes sinful nature
25. A porter in the temple
26. Masculine pronoun used 9,964 times in the Authorized Version
27. Put on the _____ of salvation
28. Story with a point
30. Believed to have burned Rome and blamed the Christians
31. "_____ up the ghost" means "died"
33. Seven sons of Sceva did this "naked and bleeding"
36. Before
38. Forbidden food
39. King of Hamath who sent his son as an emissary to David
41. "_____ my Father's house are many mansions"
44. "_____ my people . . . shall humble themselves"

PUZZLE 24

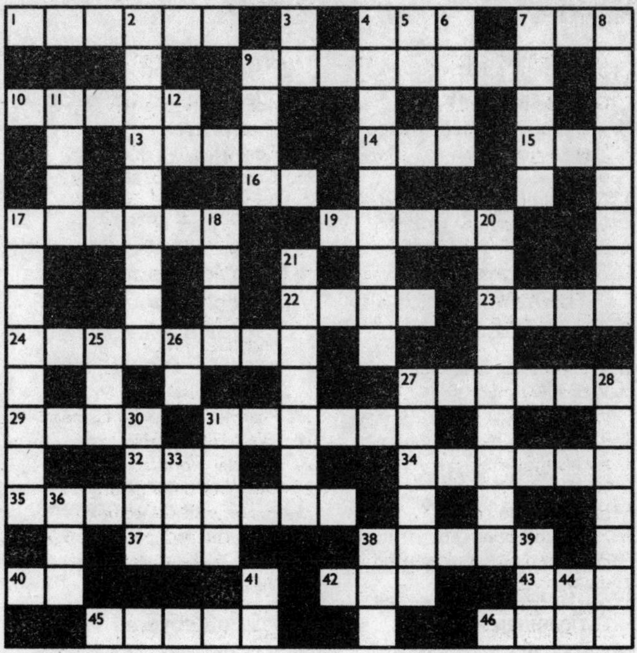

ACROSS

1. Kind of shame
4. Christian in Rome
10. Canals used to water crops
11. Pure
15. Stood still in response to Joshua's prayer
16. Sold a cave to Abraham in which he buried Sarah
19. Earth
20. Ancient name for modern Aswan, Egypt
22. Goods were moved using this method
23. Can mean "very"
24. Mosaic law determined what one could _____
26. "Youth and _____ are meaningless"
28. To have a stiff one means one is stubborn
29. Change that brings one to God
31. _____ what is evil and do good
34. Used to anoint kings
35. Disciple from Bethsaida
36. Group of livestock
37. Sent to Egypt to bring back the prophet Urijah

DOWN

2. Breaking an oath
3. Jesus raised the widow's son here
5. Mother of King Hezekiah
6. Religious festival allowing no work
7. Could describe a prophet or an evil fortune teller
8. River through Elam
9. Sea of Galilee was really a _____
12. "_____ thy presence is fulness of joy"
13. "To live is Christ, and to die is _____"
14. Ornamental carving
17. Pile
18. Shrub covered with prickly stinging hairs
19. Chief god of the Philistines
20. People of Nineveh wore this after hearing Jonah's prophecy
21. Lifespan of the human soul
25. An interval of rest or relief
27. Hebrew equivalent of our *r*

DOWN

30. Constellation mentioned in Job
32. Contained six hins
33. Elisha plowed with twenty-four
35. Hebrew equivalent of our *p*

ACROSS

1. Simon of Cyrene carried this for Jesus
5. When Israel left Egypt, there was not one _____ person among them
8. Lump of earth mentioned plurally in Job 38
9. Mound or rampart built of earth and stone
11. Swift messenger
12. "If _____ man thirst, let him come unto me, and drink"
13. Ancient land mentioned twice by the prophet Jeremiah
14. Name for a ravaging insect
16. Clouds from this direction can mean rain in Israel
19. Sometimes spelled with a "j"; heading for Psalm 119:73-80
21. Proverbs condemns a proud _____
22. Fifth month of the Hebrew year coinciding approximately with early August
24. Psalm 66 mentions the incense of _____
26. Another name for shittim wood
29. Rebelled against Abimelech
30. Price paid to free a captive
33. Means "why" and was part of Jesus' cry
34. Another name for Abijah, son of Rehoboam
36. "_____ weapon that is formed against thee shall prosper"
38. Religious ceremony
40. God "shall _____ forever"

DOWN

2. Noah saw an outpouring of this
3. Priests were to _____ a bronze pot used to cook a sin offering
4. A _____ of manna was kept in the Ark
5. Several Psalms describe God's protection from these
6. Made from rolled parchment
7. John was told to do this to a book
9. Jesus delivered her from demon possession
10. Town near Joppa where Peter ministered
14. Hebrew letter introducing Psalm 119:129-136
15. Number of special prophets who die for 3 1/2 days
17. Philistine city from where the Ark was returned to Israel
18. Egyptian god
20. Hebrew for "balsam tree"
23. Most significant god in the Canaanite pantheon
25. Can mean "to collect"
26. Time or length of life
27. Two words describing a symbol for Israel in Jeremiah 18
28. Father of Uz, Hul, Gether, and Mash
31. When Paul warned of a storm, the centurion believed the _____ of the ship
32. Israel could "_____ no fire" on the Sabbath
35. Adam's was extracted

PUZZLE 26

ACROSS

41. Rock from which minerals are extracted
44. God's anger often does this
45. To pull into pieces
47. Will melt "with fervent heat" someday; usually plural
48. Done with water in a well

DOWN

37. Zacchaeus was in one when Jesus saw him
39. "_____ not aside from following the Lord"
42. Esau's hair was this color
43. Wanted to be an eye in 1 Corinthians
46. Early Egyptian kings claimed descent from this god

ACROSS

3. Carried in the girdle
6. Tertullus was one
9. Type of tree used to make an idol
10. Saw his father's nakedness
11. Greek equivalent of English *m*
12. "_____ into his gates with thanksgiving"
14. A cattle rustler killed by the Philistines while on a raid
17. Criminal released instead of Jesus
18. Angels "laid _____" of Lot and his family
20. Nisan and Iyyar split this month
22. "_____ your hands, all ye people"
24. Very binding promise
26. We should _____ our parents' commands about our necks
28. God's will never fail
31. His son was picked to spy on the Promised Land for Manasseh
32. To be excessive in one's attention or affection

DOWN

1. Onesimus was one
2. Woman with the issue of blood touched Jesus' _____
4. Fortified city of Naphtali
5. New Testament spelling of "Ramah"
7. Can mean "to the same extent"
8. Psalmist's request was to be "_____ than snow"
13. To go against
15. Where Paul was stoned and left for dead
16. Moses' turned into a snake
17. Powerful burst of air
19. Type of tree first found after the Flood
21. To stagger
23. God _____ our sins thanks to Christ's sacrifice
25. To gain a victory
27. Endured much hardship for the sake of the gospel
28. Old word meaning "knew"
29. "_____ unto others"

ACROSS

34. At least eight varieties are listed in Scripture
36. Powerful region in northeast Africa in Bible times
38. Paul's nephew warned him of one
39. Venomous snake

DOWN

30. Chief returned with Zerubbabel from exile
31. Used to power a ship
33. Jephtha took refuge there
35. God from the _____ of the lion and bear
37. Opposite of "down"

ACROSS

1. One of Satan's many names
5. To tell about Christ
9. Covered the mountain when Moses went to speak with God
10. Old word meaning "sent forcefully"
11. Jesus' parable of the seed began with this activity
12. Wilderness through which the Israelites passed
13. Associated with Magog
15. Valley where a battle between nine kings occurred
17. _____ of the Chaldeans
18. "_____ of divination" were offered to Balaam by Balak
21. Husk; fed to swine
22. Eshcol was named after a cluster of this fruit
24. Burial places
26. Another name for algum wood
29. Writing instrument
31. Old word for "swamps"
32. A drinking vessel

DOWN

1. Eighth plague brought on Egypt
2. One from Rabbah contained a talent of gold
3. Jesus did this for two crowds in the Gospels
4. Used for corporal punishment
5. To bundle
6. Blood was sprinkled on Aaron's right "great _____"
7. Relieved
8. Tool mentioned in Isaiah 10
13. Blind men do this
14. "Curious _____ of the ephod"
15. The "clothes" Mary wrapped Jesus in
16. Area between the cherubim at the top of the Ark; two words
19. Solomon built _____ cities in Hamath
20. Place in Moab mentioned in Isaiah 15
23. Capital city of King Hadar of Edom
25. Another word for "breasts"

1
2
3
4
5
6
7
8
9
10
11
12
13
14
15
16
17
18
19
20
21
22
23
24
25
26
27
28
29
30
31
32

DOWN

27. Israelites were not to "_____ the corners of their beards"
28. Expression of emphasis, used 1,050 times as one letter in the Authorized Version
30. Between the months of Tammuz and Elul

ACROSS

1. "Princes have _____ me without cause"
9. Jephthah's was very rash
10. Partner or peer
11. "_____ of the eye"; symbol of that which is precious
12. Reubenite chief who took part in the rebellion of Korah
13. Household gods and means of divination
17. Possibly another name for the Nile
18. "The sluggard will . . . _____ in harvest"
19. Saul was "_____ wounded of the archers"
21. Jesus told the rich young ruler to do this with his possessions
23. Seat of strength and vigor
24. Ancestor of Boaz
25. God's angels will "_____ thee in all thy ways"

DOWN

2. Descendant of Gershom, son of Levi
3. Second foundation stone in the New Jerusalem
4. Sin of longing for another's possessions
5. _____ of Babel
6. Gideon asked God to use this for a sign
7. He was 912 when he died
8. Ensures that a wall is perpendicular; mentioned in Amos
12. Birds of the night mentioned in Jeremiah 50
14. His brother did not want to raise children for him
15. Container for baking
16. Isaiah 59 refers to "cockatrice' _____"
20. Another word for "forgive"
22. Four discovered an abandoned Syrian camp full of food
23. Yeast

PUZZLE 29

ACROSS

26. Jesus was the most significant one in Scripture
28. Island to which John was exiled
30. "_____ not life more than meat?"
31. Without wisdom

DOWN

24. Fully grown
27. Waste away
29. Last of the Rephaim giants

ACROSS

1. Solomon wanted to be this
3. Office in the church
8. God's response to sin
9. Old word meaning "to speak"
10. Part of the Passover meal·
11. Azariah's Babylonian name
13. Passed from father to son
14. Birds
15. "_____ of the ground made the Lord God to grow every tree"
16. "He _____ me beside still waters"
17. Another word for "idols"
18. Another word for "hell" in Greek mythology
21. Defeated Zerah the Ethiopian
23. Prophet from Moresheth
25. Used to cut down trees
26. Biblical "worm" associated with death
29. Abraham's first son

DOWN

1. Word used to pronounce judgment against something
2. Simeon and Levi avenged their _____
3. Refers to the first shoot of a plant
4. To listen to
5. Trials develop this
6. Can refer to eternity
7. Land, livestock, and valuables
11. Detestable to God
12. Part of the drink offered to Jesus
13. Man of Judah of the family of Shelah
14. Jeremiah saw these in a vision
15. "_____, let not the Lord be angry, and I will speak"
18. Joseph and Mary were registering for this when Jesus was born
19. Torn cloth often connected with filth
20. Can mean "ordained"
22. Sackcloth and _____
23. Used in sacrificial offerings

PUZZLE 30

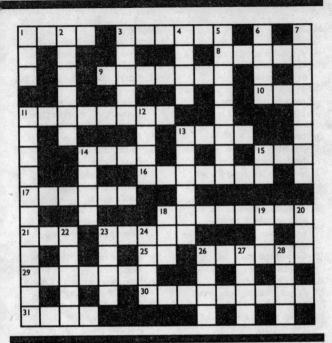

ACROSS

30. God claimed these
31. Bird's home

DOWN

24. Israel made one of gold at Sinai
26. This used to water the earth
27. Town in the territory of Benjamin asssigned to the Levites
28. Transferred Judah's capital to Samaria

ACROSS

1. Profitable for doctrine, reproof, correction, instruction in righteousness
5. Was 7 1/2 feet long on the cherubs in the temple
7. Samson was never to do this to his hair
8. Unselfish love
9. Joseph's wife, Asenath, was from here
11. Describes the crowds that came to Jesus
12. "It shall come to _____"
15. Cushi and Ahimaaz did this after Absalom's death
17. God's Holy Spirit speaks only what he _____
18. Coated the inside and outside of Noah's ark
20. Early king of Edom
23. At Jesus death, these were rent
26. Moses struck a rock with one and water gushed out
28. Solomon spoke of "the way of a man with a _____"
29. To have one forcefully shaved off was a disgrace
31. Jesus said these would cry out
32. Some believe it was the capital of Moab
33. "_____ men" or sailors
36. League of ten cities east of the Jordan
37. Jesus has the one to hell

DOWN

1. To do this with "mingled seed" violated Mosaic law
2. Father of a large family, tribe, or even a nation
3. Some scholars place this land in the north Arabian Desert
4. Flying symbol of strength
5. Very young lion or bear
6. Means "beginning"
7. False religion
10. Thessalonican Jews claimed the Christians "_____ the world upside down"
11. A plant that illustrates the power of faith; two words
13. Jether's son of the tribe of Asher
14. One of two found on the mercy seat
16. Land east of Eden; its name means "wandering"
19. Horse of warfare in Revelation was this color
21. Another word for "gift"
22. Christian faith rests on the truth that Christ is _____
24. Old word for "love"
25. After Eli's prophecy, Hannah's "countenance was no more _____"
27. Marked the eastern limit of the territory of Ahasuerus
30. "Give _____"; biblical expression for "listen"
34. Some estimate it was 450 feet long
35. May be another name for Philistine Gath

PUZZLE 31

1
2
3
4
5
6
7
8
9
10
11
12
13
14
15
16
17
18
19
20
21
22
23
24
25
26
27
28
29
30
31
32
33
34
35
36
37

ACROSS

1. One of five Midianite chieftains killed at Moses command
3. She carried a letter to the Roman Christians
6. Stringed musical instrument
7. "_____, an horror of great darkness fell upon him"
8. To separate grain
9. May be another word for "gazelle"
10. "_____ have sinned, and come short of the glory of God"
12. To change one's mind
14. Number of special trees in the Garden
17. Name of a tower
19. What Satan does to the Christian
21. Not one of Jesus' was broken
24. Roman emperor who murdered his mother
26. Evil desires
28. Jesus asked if anyone could _____ to his own height
29. "Yea, yea; _____, _____"

DOWN

1. People could not "_____" Stephen's wisdom
2. Site for sacrifices
3. Jesus told us to be "_____" like our heavenly Father
4. "Pay me what thou _____"; the ungrateful servant's demand
5. Sixth month of the Jewish year
10. John the Baptist said this was "laid unto the root"
11. "Neither shall they _____ war anymore"
13. Son of Seth
15. Long word for "sin"
16. Number of plagues brought against Egypt
18. Homes to lions
20. Vessel
22. To the exclusion of others, used 239 times in the Authorized Version
23. Abraham was asked to sacrifice his _____
25. Celebration of Christ's resurrection
27. Hooks for connecting curtains of the tabernacle

PUZZLE 32

ACROSS

31. Group such as the Sadducees or Pharisees
32. Eleventh month of the Jewish year
33. Samson tore one apart with his hands
34. Eighth son of Jacob
35. To emit a sudden copious flow

DOWN

30. To turn away
31. Another word for "psalm"

ACROSS

1. Jesus did this to Paul
5. Great warrior; his name was an early Hebrew form of "Jesus"
8. In time past
9. Moses' first cousin once removed
10. Next to the last judge of Israel
11. Jesus' command early in his ministry "_____ no man"
13. Mighty river flooding lower Egypt every year
14. Used in covenants in ancient times; Mosaic covenant also
16. Cut and shaped
18. Son of Noah from whom Israel descended
21. Judge from Zebulun who judged Israel ten years
23. God has _____ apostles, prophets, teachers . . .
25. Job's sons did this
27. Paul encouraged them to be faithful to their masters

DOWN

2. City where Paul was stoned
3. Sisera got one through the head
4. Fruit
5. Prophet who described a terrible locust plague
6. Name given to believers
7. Agur addressed proverbs to him
12. God used this to show us our sinful nature
14. Joseph saw his brothers' _____ bow down in a dream
15. God's Word is this to us
16. God sent these to help the Israelites defeat the Canaanites
17. "Eye of a _____"
19. Jesus compared himself to a _____ when he addressed Jerusalem
20. Aaron did this to gold earrings to make the golden calf
22. God compared the strength of an Amorite to these trees

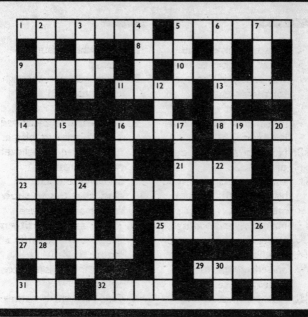

ACROSS

29. People here wanted to make a name for themselves
31. Jacob gave Esau 200
32. Sharp tool used to get large animals moving

DOWN

24. Cherubs in the temple were made of this wood
25. Ran
26. Man's first home
28. Moo
30. Several brooks went there

ACROSS

1. Living instrument of war
6. Done to some gourds for a stew
9. Refers to an "ointment" of the Holy Spirit
10. "Trees of the Lord are full of _____"
12. Judge from Gilead who judged Israel 20 years
13. Supplied according to God's "riches in glory"
15. Proclaim
17. Improper, out of place
19. City in northern Benjamin
23. "Snare, and a _____, and a stumblingblock"
24. Several Greek islands mentioned in the New Testament found here
25. To place
26. City of refuge east of Jordan in Manasseh
29. "Will a man _____ God?" Israel did through lack of tithes
30. Rich man experienced this after his death
31. To allow

DOWN

1. Created on the third day
2. Cripple did this when Peter and John prayed
3. Philip was tetrarch here
4. God sent Christ to _____ us to himself
5. Sun does by day; moon does by night
6. Called "the greater light"
7. Paul was one
8. "Keep the _____ of my lips"
11. Having an ability; used 160 times in the Authorized Version
14. One who scoffs
16. Wading bird of the heron family
18. Drawn out attack against a fortified city
20. Ruled by Sihon
21. Paul stayed at the house of Judas on "Straight _____"
22. "In _____ of hell fire"
24. Died of a severe disease in his feet
27. Falsehood
28. Used to describe traps men set for others

72

PUZZLE 34

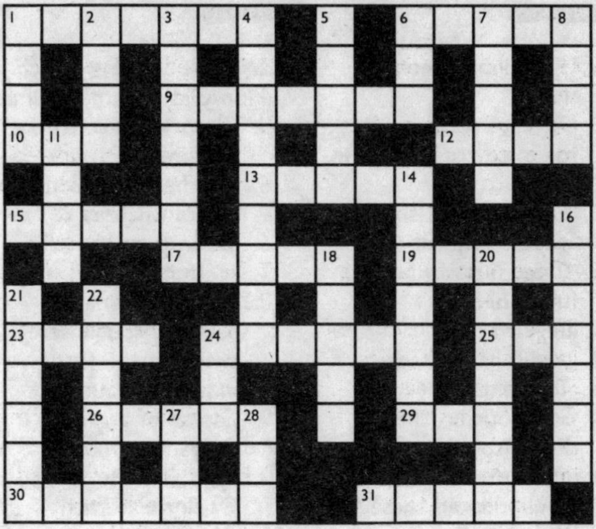
1 2 3 4 5 6 7 8 9 10 11 12 13 14 15 16 17 18 19 20 21 22 23 24 25 26 27 28 29 30 31

ACROSS

1. Joseph's brothers _____ him
3. Average amount a yoke of oxen could plow in a day
5. Nebuzaradan left these people in Judah
8. Onesimus ran away from him
11. Reward
12. Ate Jonah's shade
13. To grant favor
14. Had four brothers; Bela's son
16. Opposite of "she"
17. Paul endured these for the gospel
19. Profession of writing
20. Overseer of temple servants in Nehemiah's time
23. Common means of transportation
25. Grab suddenly
27. Inferior variety of wheat
29. Referred to a solar time keeping device
31. Figure in Greek mythology identified with Egyptian Isis

DOWN

2. Book detailing worship in Old Testament times
4. Clean when oxen are not present
5. Will be made from a sword one day
6. Syrian god
7. To loot in battle
8. Paul and Barnabas passed through here twice on the first missionary journey
9. Capital of a great Canaanite empire
10. Used as a site for jewelry placement
15. Will never happen to Christ's kingdom
18. Hard, heavy, black heartwood
20. Spared during several plagues in Egypt
21. City called "Ptolemais" in the New Testament
22. Seat used when riding an animal
24. Ancient device used to facilitate climbing
26. Records the foundation of the early church

PUZZLE 35

ACROSS

32. Plural for "thee"
33. Bird's home
34. Considered the seat of emotions

DOWN

28. Son of Ram, descendant of Judah
30. Chose good pasture for himself at his uncle's expense

ACROSS

1. Enemies
5. Rift running from Mount Hermon to the Gulf of Aqabah
8. Must be done "in spirit and in truth"
10. One of David's mighty men, also called Zalmon
11. Similar to "behold"
12. Jabin had 900 chariots of _____
13. Same as Tyre, a Phoenician port south of Sidon
14. Jesus used it as an example of his homelessness
17. Purple _____ was made from murex shellfish
18. A measure of capacity, a little less than two quarts
20. Plural form of a measurement of about 606 feet
24. Pharisees did this to Jesus' tomb
25. Tabernacle was covered with _____ skins
27. Edge of a hill
28. Famous pharaoh
29. One of four sons born to Ashur of Judah by Naarah
32. Animal that ate Jezebel
34. Bezaleel's father
36. Son of Ephraim and founder of a tribal family
38. Wading bird that was unclean food
39. Prophet who confronted Pekah's forces
40. For fear that

DOWN

1. David and Jonathan
2. "Their feet are _____ to shed blood"
3. Abram was called from here
4. God promised Abraham children as numerous as sand on a _____
5. Levite chief of eighteenth division of temple service
6. Scripture mentions about 50 varieties
7. Habakkuk used this animal's feet as an example of strength
9. Crafty
13. Title beginning eighteenth section of Psalm 119
15. Better to pluck it out than to join it in hell
16. For everything there is one
19. "_____ the rivers of Babylon"
21. Amalek's mother
22. In Jesus' parable, a king forgave one of 10,000 talents
23. Capital of Hadad, fourth king of Edom
26. Son of Baasha; ruled Israel for two years
27. Ahab called Ben-hadad this and brought a curse on himself
29. Chalcedony with colors unevenly distributed
30. Jehoram conquered the Edomites here
31. After lambda
32. Samson was from this tribe
33. Emphasis expression
35. Can mean "to deliver from"

PUZZLE 36

ACROSS

41. To _____ in the dust; sign of grief
42. Jachin and Boaz were each one

DOWN

36. Word for "work" used only four times in the Authorized Version
37. Jacob camped "beyond the tower of _____"
39. Esther was treated for six months with "_____ of myrrh"

ACROSS

1. Eleventh month of Jewish year
3. Son of Zerubbabel
6. Used once in the Authorized Version to describe fussy excitement
10. Old spelling of "hemorrhoid"
11. Spies made one to Rahab
12. Number of tribes in the northern kingdom
13. Crosswise threads in weaving
15. Generic word for God in the Semitic languages
16. Number of witnesses needed for capital punishment
17. "_____, every one that thirsteth"
19. Silver jewelry in Song of Solomon
20. Positional description used 1,536 times in the Authorized Version
22. "_____ up the gift of God"
24. For the back of a fool
25. "I will come in to him, and will _____ with him"
26. Son of Gershon
30. Killed 600 Philistines with an ox goad
32. Moses was put in one of bulrushes
33. Father of Hophni and Phinehas, evil priests
34. Amalekite king Samuel "hewed . . . into pieces"
36. Had partial charge over the Shalleketh Gate of the temple
38. Third son of Simeon
39. Son of Ulla, from the tribe of Asher
40. Moses had one of gratitude after Israel crossed the Red Sea

DOWN

1. Lazy
2. Name for second Hebrew letter and the number 2
4. Elijah was awakened by an angel and told to do this
5. Paralytic healed at Lydda by Peter's prayer
6. Bright star in the Constellation Boötes mentioned in Job
7. Requires action
8. Highly distasteful
9. Zipporah called Moses "a _____ husband"
14. God has not given us this
18. To reconcile
21. Son of Issachar
23. "This _____ now bone of my bone"
27. Descendant of Asher; son of Zophah
28. Hagar's native land
29. Means "white rumped" and may have been an addax
30. Jabin's captain
31. One of two Egyptian store cities the Israelites built
35. Man-made image of a false god
37. Son of Bigvai who returned with Ezra
41. His three sons repopulated the earth
42. Know
43. Plural first person possessive used 1,442 times in the Authorized Version
45. Designates great age; used 376 times in the Authorized Version

ACROSS

42. Our sins can be as white as this hair
44. "I am not _____, but I and the Father that sent me"
46. Aramaic paraphrases of Hebrew Scripture
47. Describes the number of Israelite children redeemed by cash because they outnumbered the Levites
48. Personal pronoun used 954 times in the Authorized Version

ACROSS

1. Wine sediments
4. Worn by mourners
9. Written by Paul to Christians in an Ionian town on the Cayster River
10. Another name for Quirinius
11. Food
13. Corrosion of iron
15. Pledge
18. Egyptian sun-god
20. Killed 1,000 Philistines with a jawbone
24. Female sheep
25. Malchiah was one
28. Title for last section of Psalm 119
29. Seat of the intellect, feelings, and will
30. Bethlehem; three words
32. Paul was stoned here
34. Jews still look for one
36. Waste
39. David and Samson killed one of these
40. One of the Nethinim mentioned in Ezra 2
41. The rock where Samson lived after a slaughter of Philistines
42. Ezekiel saw a valley of _____ bones
43. Popular name for the celebration of Christ's birth

DOWN

2. Another word for "jealousy"
3. Angels told Lot they would sleep there
4. A copier of manuscripts
5. A Roman emperor
6. Plant of the lily family
7. "He sent his word, and _____ them"
8. Affirmative reply
10. Name meaning "Anointed One"; three words
12. They use a staff and a sling
14. Abbreviation for two books in the O.T.
16. A city of Moab
17. Bad
19. Youngest son of Noah
21. Hidden
22. What Goliath said when David's stone hit him
23. Entrapping device
26. Progeny
27. Son of King Saul
30. Dromedary and Bactrian are two varieties
31. Two words spoken on several occasions by angels to frightened people
33. "Thou, Lord, only makest me dwell in _____"
35. Four possible sites are offered for this famous mountain
37. "Salute one another with an holy _____"
38. God did this to the ark's door
41. Eldest son of Judah

PUZZLE 38

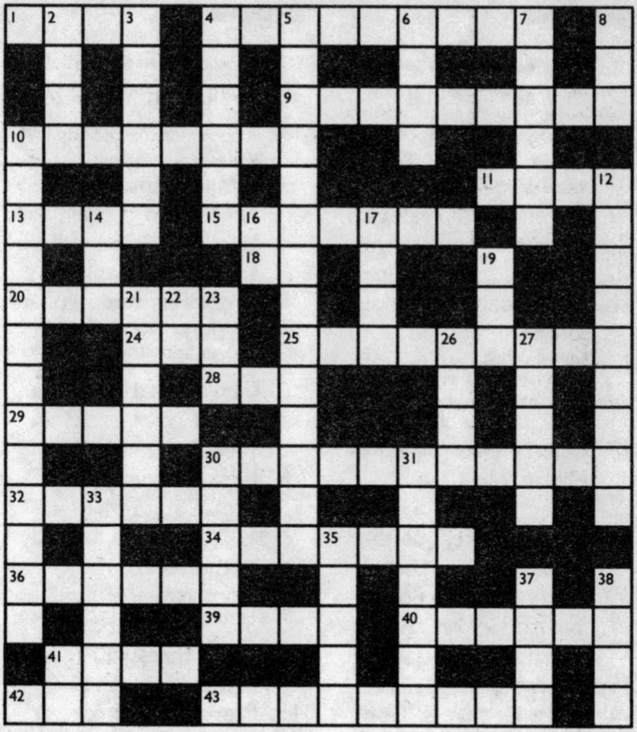

ACROSS

1. Streets of the New Jerusalem are this
7. For centuries, it was the capital of the known world
9. Apostles were released from one by an angel
10. "Walk _____ the Spirit"
11. Jesus raised the widow's son here
12. When God said Sarah would have a son: "_____ year"
13. One of two princes of Midian killed by Gideon's men
16. Signifies "like," used 3,369 times in the Authorized Version
17. Type of soldier that wounded King Saul
19. "There is none _____ but one, that is, God"
21. "A _____ man is unstable in all his ways"
24. "Let not the sun _____ down upon your wrath"
26. Their five cities were Ashdod, Gaza, Ashkelon, Gath, and Ekron

DOWN

1. _____ of Ethiopia; mentioned in Job 28
2. "_____ in me, and I in you"
3. Satan tempted Jesus to jump from the temple's
4. Like silver, God will do this to his people
5. Amos lists the numbers of these by different countries
6. God's word to Gideon, "Have not I _____ thee?"
8. Nebuchadnezzar's dream statue had a _____ of iron and clay in the feet
14. Hometown of medium Saul visited, about seven miles from Nazareth
15. Prevents an arrow or spear from being withdrawn
18. To tear apart
20. Jesus cast seven out of Mary Magdalene
22. Place near Sodom and Gomorrah
23. Some type of vegetable eaten by the poor

ACROSS

29. "Thou hast the _____ of thy youth"
31. Refers to conflict; used 225 times in the Authorized Version
32. Jesus' were called parables
33. "_____ to and fro, and carried about with every wind of doctrine"

DOWN

25. Greek word for hell
27. Type
28. One of two on a sharp sword
30. "_____ am I, O Lord God?" David's question

ACROSS

1. Where our Savior died
4. Wife of Hosea
8. Bird of beauty, but unclean to eat
10. Flash
13. "_____, O Lord, thou knowest it altogether"
14. Used in perfumes, as a medicine, and as incense
17. Part of the foot
18. "_____" Lord God! behold, thou hast made the heaven and the earth"
19. He "sendeth _____ on the just and on the unjust"
21. Wicked Israelites burned incense to the _____ of heaven
22. Married two Hittite women which caused his parents grief
25. One's lifelong companion
26. A village NW of Hebron
28. Ancestor of Jesus
29. Samson lost his
30. "Ye _____ be born again"
31. What the father gave his returning prodigal son

DOWN

1. "_____ him"
2. Jacob made one at Bethel
3. "They shall _____, and not be weary"
4. Sea of Tiberias, also called Sea of _____
5. A plant used in cookery
6. City of seven hills
8. 3,630 of his descendants returned from captivity
10. "Thy _____ hath made me great"
11. A variation of Nun, father of Joshua
12. The firmament
15. Prefix meaning "joint"
16. Letters
20. Poison of a snake
21. Calm
23. Compass point
24. God is the Alpha and Omega, the _____ to _____
25. "Desire the sincere _____ of the word"
27. Near

PUZZLE 40

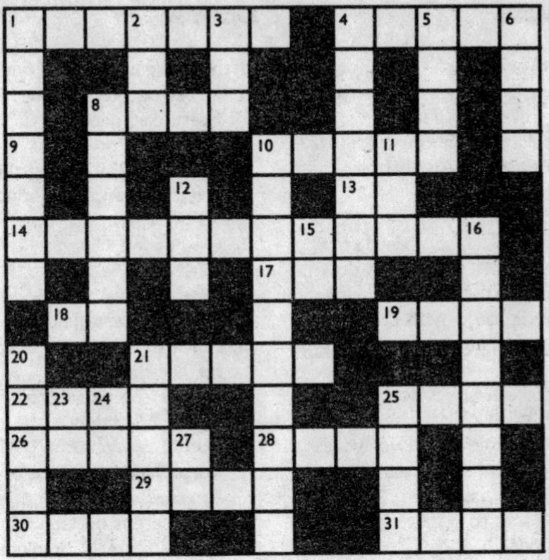

ACROSS

1. Son of Ram
3. Was fixed between the good and evil after death
5. Feminine pronoun, used 1,022 times in the Authorized Version
9. Mournful cry
10. Lack of _____ forced four men to let their friend down through the roof
11. Having to do with divination
12. "_____ not one against another"
13. Signalled Peter's denial of Christ
14. Jesus cursed one; two words
16. Country that refused the Israelites passage
17. "It came to _____"; happened
20. Feast
22. Heber's father
24. Originally a religious caste among the Persians
25. Egyptian city also called No Amon
26. Where Moses struck a rock for water
28. "Their _____ is the poison of dragons"
31. Land bought with the money of Jesus' betrayal; two words
33. Moses face did this
34. Nabal was one
35. Clean animals chewing this had to divide the hoof

DOWN

1. Worship or belief in one God
2. Heber pitched his tent here; Sisera died here
3. "Place of a skull"
4. The seventh stone on the high priest's breastplate (jacinth RSV)
6. One of five Midianite kings killed with Balaam
7. Were iron in Nebuchadnezzar's dream
8. Christian lady at Joppa known for her charity
9. First person plural pronoun, used 1,772 times in the Authorized Version
13. Joseph hid a silver one in Benjamin's sack
14. Says there is no God
15. Jerusalem's wall completely rebuilt in this month
18. Bribed Ben-hadad to break his league with Baasha
19. Ointment with which Mary anointed Jesus
21. Ancestor of Jesus, the grandfather of Zerubbabel
23. _____ of the Lord, figurative of personal intervention
24. Done with a short sickle in Bible times
27. Offered a wrong sacrifice and died with Nadab
29. Tenth letter of the Hebrew alphabet
30. Word for God in the Semitic languages
32. Name meaning "life" or "living"

PUZZLE 41

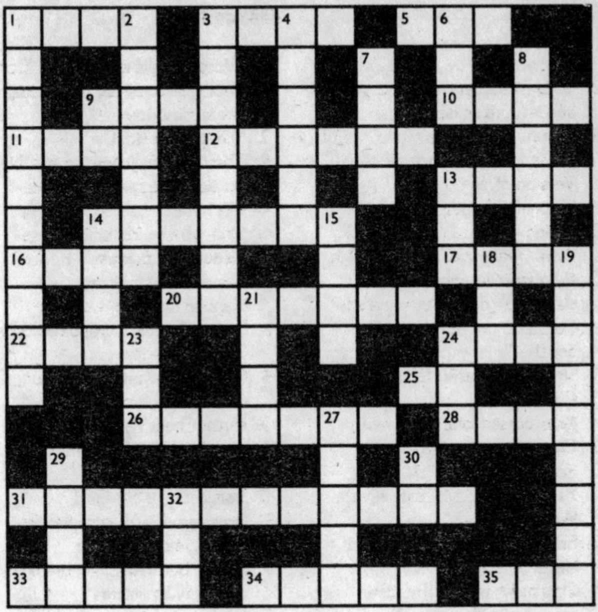

ACROSS

1. Name given by Hiram of Tyre to a district in northern Galilee
5. "I will make you _____ of men"
7. Satan is the "prince of the power of the _____"
8. Cruel wilderness bird
11. Called Ebal in Hebrew; an early Arab, son of Joktan
12. Abraham bought Sarah's grave site from the descendants of _____
14. Serpent's false promise, "Ye shall not surely _____"
15. Aroma
16. Naomi's faithful Moabite daughter-in-law
19. Elisha received Elijah's
21. Priest involved in moving the Ark
23. Son of Uriah who weighed silver and gold
24. Pharaoh's butler dreamed about this
26. Son of Nebo
27. Jesus is the bright and morning _____
28. Family of temple servants who returned from captivity
29. "Joshua" was an early form of this name
32. Abimelech destroyed Shechem and scattered this over it
33. About 3,000 people were on one when Samson brought the house down

DOWN

1. Temple walls had "_____ figures of cherubims . . . palm trees . . . flowers"
2. Town close to Bethel
3. "_____ shall betray _____ to death"
4. "Whose shoe's _____ I am not worthy to unloose"
5. Old expression for "poker faced"; "set my face like _____"
6. Some believers were martyred with this
9. "_____, every one that thirsteth"
10. Only Christ offers this
13. Used for the first time in Genesis 13:9 in the Authorized Version
15. Aaron made the Israelites "naked unto their _____"
17. Animal fat from animals dying naturally could be "_____" but not eaten
18. Banished persons
20. Killed a giant
22. Two words; is the lowest point on earth at 1,292 feet below sea level
25. In Jesus' parable, a man sold all he had for one
30. Father of Eliphal, one of David's mighty men
31. Egyptian pharaoh who made an alliance with Hoshea

PUZZLE 42

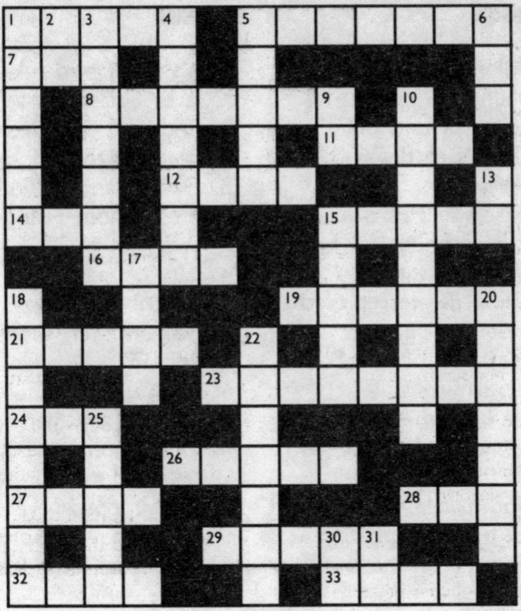

ACROSS

1. Solomon brought this animal to Israel
2. Scene of two of David's battles with the Philistines
4. Isaac asked Esau to take one and hunt for him
5. Another spelling for the tenth letter of the Hebrew alphabet
8. Head of a clan of Benjamin
9. He blessed Abraham
10. Climbing plant related to the grape
11. God makes the sun rise on these people too
12. Created on the third day
13. Ingredient in special tabernacle perfume
15. Jesus is this
17. Third king of Judah
18. A metallic device that alternated with pomegranates on high priest's hem
20. Priest in David's time
21. Naaman was from there
23. Abigail rode out to meet David on one

DOWN

1. Name of two rulers over Galilee
2. Jesus and two thieves crucified there
3. Descendant of Reuben after whom a stone was named
4. City of Judah
5. Describes the way to hell; another word for "broad"
6. Term used by Paul to describe a helper
7. One who attempts to tell the future
9. Paul stopped here on his journey to Rome
14. Nathanael came from there
16. God gave man this over animals
18. False god whose priests Elijah contested
19. People here thought Paul and Barnabas were gods
20. Jerahmeelite
21. Philistine giant killed by one of David's men
22. Another word for deer
25. Stand _____ in the faith

ACROSS

24. Early Gadite
25. Used to separate wheat
26. Christian woman living in Rome known to Paul
29. Each gate of the New Jerusalem is one
30. Youngest son of Jacob

DOWN

27. When fleeing from Saul, David got provisions here
28. Opposite of out; used 14,130 times in the Authorized Version

ACROSS

1. Custodian of a royal harem
5. Mountain in Samaria opposite Mt. Gerizim
7. Dedicated or set apart for worship of God
9. Sixth son of Jesse
10. Peter was doing this with his hand when explaining his escape
13. Another word for "sundown"
15. Modern expression for pride
16. Annual flooding of this river has fertilized Egypt for centuries
18. Used during Old Testament divorce proceedings
19. God
21. Cared for David in his old age
23. Jacob buried idols from his family under one
25. Nehemiah refused an invitation to go there
27. Psalm 58 asks that the wicked pass away like this animal melts
29. One who attempts to converse with the dead
34. Aaron and _____ held up Moses' hands
37. Means "planted"; used 32 times in the Authorized Version
39. One of the things amputated on Adoni-zedek
40. Chosen to oversee practical services in the church
42. In Nathan's parable the poor man had one that was stolen and eaten
43. Eternity has none

DOWN

1. Descendant of Seir the Horite
2. City lying about 400 miles south of Cairo
3. Burial place of judge Jair
4. Got up; used 174 times in the Authorized Version
5. Jeremiah prophesied this country's destruction
6. Jesus is this; three words
8. Spirit being who carries out God's orders
11. One of two men who survived their generation and entered Canaan
12. Captain of the guard who arrested Jeremiah
14. Anatomical area mentioned 59 times in the Authorized Version
15. High priest's sacred vestment
17. His family was cursed for their wickedness as priests
20. Denotes movement; used 1,479 times in the Authorized Version
21. Southern city of Judah, then of Simeon, then of priests
22. Serious
24. Immediately; used twice in the Authorized Version
26. Amorite allied with Abram
28. After "Imri" in a complete concordance of the Authorized Version
30. Her sister-in-law was Orpah
31. To masticate; used three times in the Authorized Version
32. Illustrates the Christian life
33. Belshazzar saw one writing

PUZZLE 44

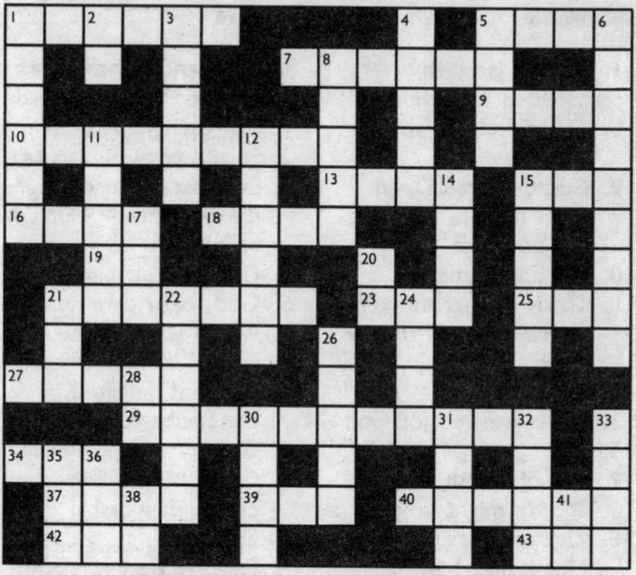

DOWN

35. To employ the function of
36. Disciples did this without success in the storm
38. Comes after "wayside" in a complete concordance of the Aurhorized Version
41. Heliopolis

ACROSS

1. King of Jarmuth defeated by Joshua
5. Achan and his family were
9. God delivered David from the _____ of the lion and bear
10. Hophni's father
11. Costly gum resin from several types of thorny shrub
12. Judah's son
13. Hebrew name for God
15. Has
17. Son of Ikkesh; one of David's mighty men
18. City or district of Moab; may have been the capital
20. Last of the annual sacred festivals under Old Testament law
23. Exclamation
24. Working animal
26. Daughter of Solomon
30. Sixth son of Joktan
32. Used to move a boat
33. Precious stone mentioned 11 times in the Authorized Version
34. His son Eleazar was the second of David's mighty men

DOWN

1. One who stands in for another; modern word expressing Jesus' task
2. Fortified city of Naphtali
3. Expression of encouragement meaning "Our Lord comes!"
4. Caleb's concubine
5. God told Adam he would labor and _____
6. Son of Ishmael whose clan was defeated by the Reubenites
7. God
8. Goddess with a great center of worship in Ephesus
14. Deep respect for God
16. Jesus called God _____
19. Isaiah prophesied that a "_____ of Jesse" would rule
20. 20, then 15 of these were measured before Paul's shipwreck
21. David's Ishmaelite camel driver
22. King of Egypt during Ahaz's reign
25. Identified with Ahasuerus
27. Forgiveness
28. Name meaning "noble"

94

ACROSS

36. "Wizards that _____, and that mutter"
37. Another name for Mt. Hermon
39. Nothing; used 36 times in the Authorized Version
40. Brother of Mamre the Amorite

DOWN

31. Expression of support
33. Defenders of Ai left the city _____
35. Town near the Valley of the Craftsmen
38. Emphatic expression, used 38 times in the Authorized Version

ACROSS

2. Little is known of Jesus'
8. An appeal to God to witness truth or bind a promise
9. Son of Joktan
11. John I describes Jesus as this to the world
12. Egyptian city
13. To want
15. Valley
16. Taught the law after the return of the exiles
17. Job 39 mentions the ostrich's in the plural
19. His son supplied Solomon's household with food one month a year
20. Jephthah fled to this place
22. To decay or waste away
24. David put five stones here
26. Elijah left in one
27. Falsehood
29. Solomon sought this
30. Giant father of Anak
31. Smell
33. Title
35. Flesh of an animal
36. Species
37. Son _____ God
38. Spell
39. God sent two of this animal in response to Elisha's curse
40. An expression of surprise or joy

DOWN

1. Used to guide animals
2. Restraining device familiar to Paul
3. Lazy
4. Knife
5. Opposite of in; used 2,696 times in the Authorized Version
6. Nebuchadnezzar set up his golden image here
7. Jesus performed his first miracle here
10. "_____, I am with you alway"
14. Person who carved two memorial stones for Aaron's shoulders
15. Paul was called one
18. Chief prince of Meshech and Tubal
19. Fifth letter of the Hebrew alphabet
20. To work hard
21. Cast Joram's body into Naboth's vineyard
23. Expanse of sky surrounding the earth
25. His sons died carrying the Ark into battle
26. Achan stole a _____ of gold
28. Jesus _____ the Son of God
29. Israel did this in the wilderness for 40 years
30. Head of a family of the Nethinim
31. Used 461 times in the Authorized Version; means "a different one"
32. Place east of Moab where Israel set up camp
34. To ridicule

PUZZLE 46

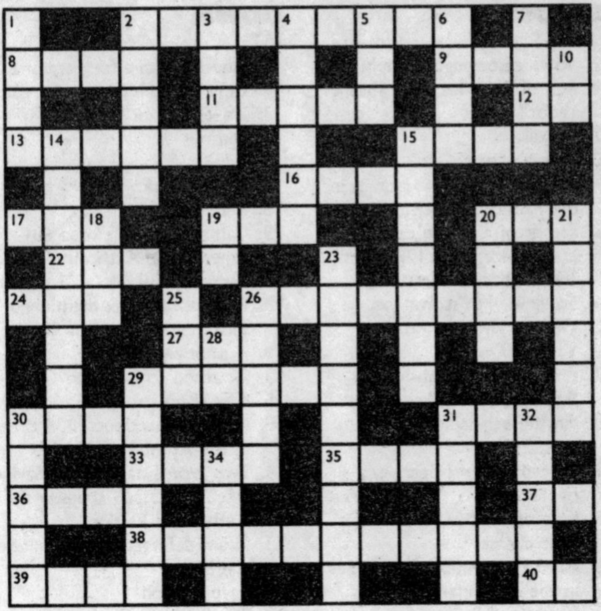

ACROSS

1. Town belonging to Naphtali
4. Son of Ram; his name means "root"
7. To kill
10. Joshua's father
11. To allow; used 1,483 times in the Authorized Version
13. Father of a clan in Ephraim
14. Looked for; used 125 times in the Authorized Version
16. To view with scorn; used twice in the Authorized Version
17. Brook where Elijah hid during first part of Israel's drought
20. "In the beginning God _____"
21. Fenced city of Naphtali; hyphenated
25. King of Judah who died of a foot disease
26. In Moab; mentioned six times in the Authorized Version
28. Brother of Buz
29. Received training from Aquila and Priscilla
33. Nebuchadnezzar saw a tree in one
35. Jesus forgave the adulteress caught "in the very _____"
37. Fifteenth letter of the Hebrew alphabet
38. Chewed by ruminants
39. Historically used in art to designate saintly biblical characters
41. Type of wood used in musical instruments

DOWN

2. Another name for Ecbatana, capital of the Medes
3. Traveler's resting place
4. Did not die
5. God
6. To give back
8. Refers to aloes
9. Can mean "still"; used 681 times in the Authorized Version
12. Pedal appendage; mentioned six times singularly in the Authorized Version
13. Attached to a curtain
15. City given to Asher
18. Number mentioned 808 times in the Authorized Version
19. Two words naming our Savior
22. Like; used 3,369 times in the Authorized Version
23. Joram defeated the Edomites there
24. Egyptian god
27. Sacrificial animal
30. Crippled
31. Tree mentioned 15 times in the Authorized Version
32. Satan
34. Plain along the border of Benjamin
36. Twelfth month of the Babylonian calendar
37. Heavy with moisture
40. Rehoboam's son
43. Priest in Jeremiah's time
45. "The _____ of the Lord are upon the righteous"
46. Respectful address

ACROSS

42. Kind of torch
44. Descendant of Esau
46. Israelite camp
49. Repaired Jerusalem's wall next to the "fish gate"
50. Her name meant "gazelle"

DOWN

47. Comes after "Asyncritus" in a complete Authorized Version concordance
48. Word used for in, on, or near

ACROSS

1. David wrongfully desired her
6. Eleventh month of the Jewish year
7. Another name for the Antichrist
8. Israelites complained that they missed these from Egypt
12. Opposite of bottom; used 91 times in the Authorized Version
13. Company of four soldiers; these guarded Peter
15. "Clear as _____"; describes the river of life
17. One opposing the gospel is compared to this animal
20. To make new again, as in the new birth
22. God expects us to do this for our needs
24. Feeling in the ears of those desiring false doctrine
26. Common name for Medo-Persian rulers
28. Used to snag fish
29. A plant with edible seeds belonging to the pea family
31. Jesus figuratively advised that it be plucked out
32. To throw; mentioned twice in the Authorized Version
34. Positive response
35. Denotes a state of existence; used 6,758 times in the Authorized Version
36. Vehicle of war
37. To eat

DOWN

1. To erase, "_____ out"
2. Paul took more than one
3. Wilderness, city, infraction of God's law
4. Boundary stone between Benjamin and Judah
5. Saul almost defeated David here, but Philistine attack intervened
6. _____ the cross
7. Insects referred to plurally three times in the Authorized Version
9. Name for Thebes
10. Shape used a lot in Solomon's house
11. Held the tongs used in cleaning the wicks of tabernacle lamps; two words
14. False god
15. One was rent from top to bottom in the temple
16. Noah's eldest son
18. Taken to clean the body
19. Near Israel's last camp in Egypt
21. Greek letter corresponding to our p
23. Hawks
25. Firepan
27. God did this on the seventh day
29. The first Jacob married
30. Seer and prophet who also wrote books about Israel's kings
33. Joshua's prayer halted its progress
34. Another word for "you"; used 3,780 times in the Authorized Version

PUZZLE 48

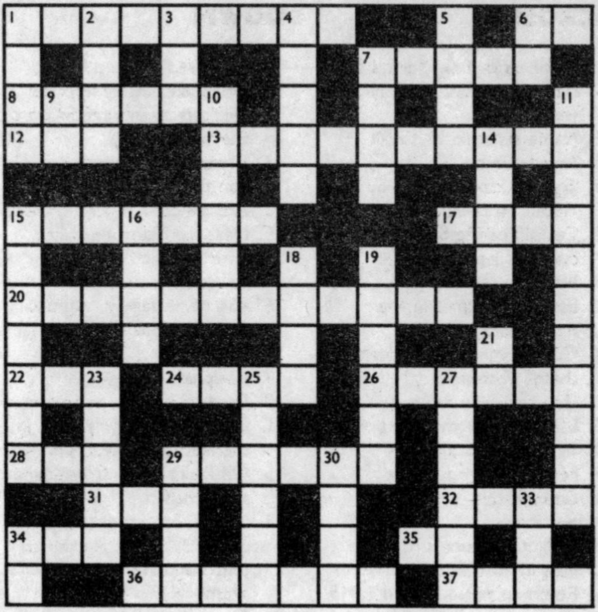

ACROSS

2. Prophets of Baal did this to themselves during a praying frenzy
5. Name given to Hananiah
9. Son of Simon
10. Type of food brought by Abigail to David
12. Captain of the Syrian army cured of leprosy
13. Negative response and a city; used 1,377 times in the Authorized Version
14. God promised to "redeem (Israel) with a stretched out _____"
16. Landmark on the east border of the Promised Land
17. Feminine pronoun used 1,022 times in the Authorized Version
18. Golgotha refers to this
20. To gather after the harvest
21. Refers to options; used 1,015 times in the Authorized Version
22. Cutting tool
23. "_____, one born in my house is mine heir"
25. Border or edge of the tabernacle curtain to which loops were attached
28. Eleventh month of Jewish year
29. Can mean "in the same way"
30. Seas, waters, enemies, and a bear do this in Scripture
32. Weapon; Goliath's had a staff like a weaver's beam
34. Son of Benjamin
35. Egyptian god

DOWN

1. To spread the good news
2. Mountains jutting into the Mediterranean directly west of the Sea of Galilee
3. Abram's early home
4. Son of Eliphaz, brother of Amalek
5. Meat from an animal killed with this method was not to be eaten
6. 454 of his family returned with Zerubbabel
7. Associate high priest with Caiaphas
8. Used to kill Sisera
11. Comfort; used only once in the Authorized Version
15. On Paul's route from Ephesus to Jerusalem
19. "Many that are first shall be _____"
23. John's action in his mother's womb
24. Obeyed
25. Isaiah saw these six winged creatures
26. Word usually applied to God; appears 7,738 times in the Authorized Version
27. One of the cities defeated by Joshua listed in Joshua 12
31. To go without food as an aid in prayer
32. Wicked city destroyed by God; Lot's home
33. Another name for the Egyptian god of the sun
35. To bring back to life
36. One who bears false witness

PUZZLE 49

ACROSS

36. Same as Luke
37. Sacrificial bird
38. Descendant of Simeon, father of Ziza
40. Impersonal pronoun used 6,875 times in the Authorized Version
41. Group associated with the Persians
42. Large groups of people descended from Israel's sons

DOWN

39. Seventeenth letter of the Hebrew alphabet

ACROSS

1. What the two witnesses in Revelation did
6. Jacob wrestled there
9. To run from
10. Path or method; used 661 times in the Authorized Version
11. To speak; used 24 times in the Authorized Version
12. Name meaning "watcher"
13. "A time to rend, and a time to _____"
15. Jacob's favorite wife
18. Guides
19. Place in Moab
21. Jesus did this for everyone
22. Moses met God there
24. Old word for "knob"
25. His pride reduced him to an animal's existence
30. Noah's temporary home
31. Written by Luke as an early history of the church
32. "_____ still, and know that I am God"

DOWN

2. God's free gift to mankind
3. First woman
4. Evil one
5. Gideon asked God to keep this off the ground
6. Luke was one
7. Series of carvings on tops of temple pillars
8. Sea of Galilee was really a _____
14. God
16. Past tense of "have"; used 3,002 times in the Authorized Version
17. God put him to death
20. To let live
22. Musical instrument listed in Daniel
23. Son of Caleb
26. Vessel used for washing
27. _____ of the Chaldees
28. David's brother
29. Eleventh letter of the Hebrew alphabet
34. Ancient Canaanite coastal city about eight miles north of Caesarea

ACROSS

33. Seer who had visions against Jeroboam
36. Stinging insect
37. Only female judge of Israel

DOWN

35. Can express complaint, grief, malicious joy, regret, and ridicule

ACROSS

1. "Godly _____ worketh repentance"
4. Joseph told the baker "birds shall _____ thy flesh"
5. Old past tense of "to wear"
8. King Elah of Israel was murdered in this man's house
10. Amorite name of Mt. Hermon
12. Jesus is called the "_____ of David"
13. Can mean "to test"
14. Left Paul and Barnabas, but later matured
16. "_____ and morning star"
19. Mountain where Balak took the prophet Balaam
21. Pungent smell
23. Used to harvest grain
27. Crown
30. Native of Arba; one of David's mighty men was one
31. Rich man asked that Lazarus do this with his finger
32. Donkey

DOWN

2. Pungent bitter plant used as a medicine
3. Armed conflict
4. Created by God "in the beginning"
6. Industrious insect praised in Scripture
7. Israel was enslaved here for 400 years
9. Led wise men to Christ
10. Jonah was thrown from one
11. Called "a mighty hunter"
15. There was no _____ in the inn
17. Sick
18. Masculine pronoun used 9,964 times in the Authorized Version
20. Raised Samuel in the temple
22. Kind of sleep Adam experienced when God made Eve
24. Traders
25. "Friend" who criticized Job
26. Means "the end"
27. Appointed to serve in the church

PUZZLE 51

ACROSS

34. First recorded polygamist
35. One put away from his fellowmen
37. Second church Jesus dictated a letter to in Revelation
38. Cliff where Jehoshaphat received a victory from God

DOWN

28. Descendant of a grandson of Benjamin
29. Affirmative response
32. Book of the church's early history
33. To kill
36. Chopping instrument

ACROSS

1. "_____, I am with you alway"
3. She and her husband were killed by God
6. Greek m
7. Number denoting singularity and used 1,898 times in the Authorized Version
9. "Sorrowful Way"; traditional route of Jesus' journey to the cross; two words
12. To publish abroad
13. To ransom; what Christ did for mankind
15. Descendant of Jeduthun; chief of a Levitical choir
16. Word describing skinny cattle in Pharaoh's dream
17. Fatal epidemic
21. Porter of the east entrance to the tabernacle in David's reign
23. Jahzerah's son; a priest
24. Object Ezekiel saw in his vision
25. Laban's oldest daughter
28. Opposite of "out"; used 14,130 times in the Authorized Version
29. Cain wandered there
30. Projectiles used in ancient warfare
31. Sandbars off the coast of Africa

DOWN

1. Brass basin used for priests' cleansing in tabernacle
2. Partially digested ruminant food
3. Roman proconsul of Cyprus
4. "Casting all your care upon him; for _____ careth for you"
5. The Council saw that Stephen's face was like that of an _____
6. Plant credited with aphrodisiac qualities
7. Hebrew word translated "eternal"
8. Negative response and an Egyptian city
10. Grandfather of Saul and Abner
11. Young man
14. Judah's eldest son
17. Part of the tops of the temple pillars
18. Indefinite article used 6,875 times in the Authorized Version
19. "The Lord is high above all _____"
20. "Give not . . . slumber to thine _____"
21. Landmark describing place where King Joash was murdered
22. "We shall reap, if we _____ not"
24. "Whom shall I send, and _____ will go for us?"
26. Third son of Shelah, son of Judah
27. Thought by some to be Moab's capital
28. Name meaning "watcher"

PUZZLE 52

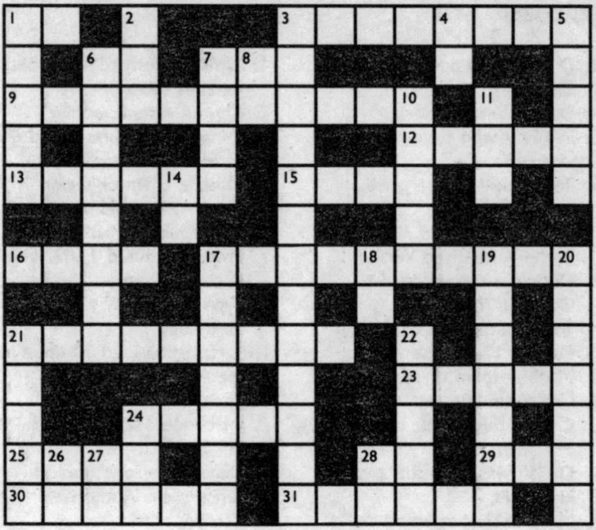
1
2
3
4
5
6
7
8
9
10
11
12
13
14
15
16
17
18
19
20
21
22
23
24
25
26
27
28
29
30
31

ACROSS

1. Dry measure containing about one quart
3. David's instrument
5. Evil king who stole Naboth's vineyard
9. Tower near where Jacob camped
12. Means "yes"; used 332 times in the Authorized Version
13. Disciple who witnessed to Cornelius' household
14. To encourage strongly
16. Eternity hasn't one
17. Moabite town or region
19. Can mean "flowed"
20. One of the highest mountains in Samaria
22. Delilah was from this area
23. Heliopolis
25. Made of shittim wood and covered with gold
27. To boil (KJV)
28. Aram's son
29. Israel told to do this at Jericho
30. "Thou shalt not muzzle the _____ when he treadeth out the corn"
31. Three went in, but Nebuchadnezzar saw four
34. Woman with the issue of blood touched Jesus' _____
35. "I have suffered . . . loss . . . that I may _____ Christ"
37. Clean animals that chewed this had to divide the hoof
38. Allow
39. Jesus healed a blind man here
41. "_____ the mouth of two or three witnesses"

DOWN

1. Christ performed numerous miracles there
2. City on Ashur's border
3. What God said he would do to Pharaoh's heart
4. Moabite town or region
6. With Aaron held up Moses' hands during a battle
7. Preposition used 2,602 times in the Authorized Version
8. Type of armor
10. Held lions
11. Exclamation used 10 times in the Authorized Version
15. Pitch
18. Introduces Psalm 119:153-160
21. For fear that
22. Denotes sorrow; used 11 times in the Authorized Version
24. "To hate is to be a liar; to _____ is to be a fool"
26. Where the Israelites lived in Egypt
30. Jezebel's father-in-law
32. Female sheep
33. Old spelling for soda deposits around Egyptian alkali lakes
36. Exclamation used 18 times in the Authorized Version
37. Tall woody grass or reed
38. To cut off
39. "_____ me come unto thee on the water"
40. To inquire; used 109 times in the Authorized Version

1		2		3	4				5	6		7		8
		9	10					11				12		
13						14					15			
		16									17	18		
19				20			21		22					
			23											24
25					26		27					28		
			29							30				
31	32	33					34							
	35					36						37		
38				39					40					
			41											
42					43						44			

ACROSS

42. Legally defend; "_____ my cause"
43. Father of a race of giants
44. Not a Gentile

ACROSS

1. An impediment to belief; two words
7. To sever; word is used 319 times in the Authorized Version
8. Part of Proverbs attributed to this king
11. "The body is _____, and hath many members"
12. Refers to moral failure; used 440 times in the Authorized Version
13. Color of ram's skins used in tabernacle construction
15. To kill
16. Son of Matthias in Jesus' genealogy
18. To rend
20. Negative response used 1,377 times in the Authorized Version
21. Would tear their clothes and wear sackcloth and ashes
24. Building referred to in Job 39
26. "_____ my sheep"
27. Early deacon
29. "Greater light to rule the day"
30. "Give unto the Lord the glory _____ unto his name"
31. King of Midian killed by Israelites
32. Peter's response when asked if Jesus paid taxes
33. People who lived near the Tigris in Ezekiel's day
34. Name that symbolizes relation between Israel and God
35. Number mentioned 242 times in the Authorized Version; number of commandments

DOWN

1. Musical instrument
2. To speak
3. Town in Judah; exact site uncertain
4. Another name for Hosea
5. Boaz's unnamed rival
6. Tithe
8. Guided; used 68 times in the Authorized Version
9. Father of Palal
10. "Charity"
14. To do wrong
15. Abraham saw this after God's destruction of the cities of the plain
16. God has "made known unto us the _____ of his will"
17. Preposition or part of a verb used 14,112 times in the Authorized Version
19. First high priest of Israel
22. Fifth son of Jesse
23. "Take thine _____, eat, drink, and be merry"
25. Another word for spirit
26. One was named Jabbok
28. Jesus raised a widow's son here
29. "The trees of the Lord are full of _____"

PUZZLE 54

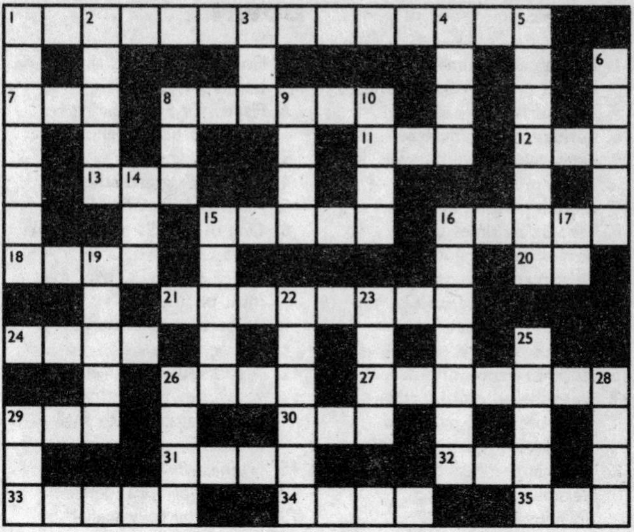

ACROSS

1. Elkanah and Hannah's son
4. "Satan . . . provoked David to _____ Israel"
8. Levitical city in Manasseh
9. Sisera hid in one, but was murdered there
10. Second person plural pronoun; used 3,780 times in the Authorized Version
11. Used to make mortar
12. Preposition used 8,122 times in the Authorized Version
14. Unit of measure
15. Another name for Addar
17. Hard-shelled reproductive body produced by a bird
19. Opposite of quiet; used 60 times in the Authorized Version
21. To permit
25. Moses' _____ became a symbol of God's power
26. Name for God conjugated with other words to describe him
27. "_____ I was with Moses, so I will be with thee"
29. Introduces Psalm 119:129-136
30. Came to Jesus by night
33. Defeated Zerah the Ethiopian
34. Material strewn throughout a valley in Ezekiel's vision
37. Feminine possessive pronoun used 1,630 times in the Authorized Version
38. Paul was "forbidden of the Holy Ghost" to preach there

DOWN

1. God "hast _____ all the borders of the earth"
2. Played for Elisha during his prophecy before Jehoshaphat
3. Tertullus was one
4. King Saul's grandfather
5. Abraham's homeland
6. One of David's mighty men from Gad
7. "He that _____ over men must be just"
11. His sons were beaten by a demoniac
12. Associated with Ithiel
13. "_____ weapon that is formed against thee shall prosper"
15. Jakeh's son
16. Jericho's principal defense
18. "Upon thy belly shalt thou _____"
20. "As ye would that men should _____ to you . . ."
22. "God _____ thee these forty years"
23. Expression of disaster
24. To bring to life
28. Jesus still bears several
29. Israel's second camp after Sinai
30. Prophet from Elkosh
31. "Valley of the shadow of _____"
32. His son helped Nehemiah rebuild Jerusalem
35. Giant king
36. Land settled by Esau's descendants

ACROSS

40. Divine One
41. Preposition, used first in Genesis 1:14 in the Authorized Version
42. Another name for Ir
45. Egyptian city
46. "The heart of fools is in the house of _____"
47. Balaam's spoke

DOWN

39. "As he thinketh in his heart, _____ is he"
43. Egyptian god
44. Form of "to be" and an interrogative; used 6,092 times in the Authorized Version

ACROSS

1. Unit of measure derived from the length of a hand
4. After Absalom's rebellion, one was sent to David to help him return to Jerusalem
7. "In _____ there is no remembrance of thee"
11. "In the night _____ of Moab is laid waste"
12. Molech, Chemosh, Ashtoreth, and Baal are examples
13. Seraphim have six
14. Daniel saw one in his vision
15. "_____ are the peacemakers"
18. Jesus got away from the multitudes and did this
20. Comes after "and" in the Appendix to Strong's Exhaustive Concordance
21. None on the New Earth
22. Earth was flooded in Noah's 600th
23. Aaron crafted this idol; two words
29. Younger brother of Judah's King Abijah
31. "I _____ no pleasant bread"
33. "Enlarge thy baldness as the _____"
35. Abimelech's command: "Draw thy sword, and _____ me"
37. Verb found for the first time in Genesis 1:11 in the Authorized Version
38. To enjoy the benefits of; used only one in the Authorized Version
40. "I _____ thee"; can refer to requests between people

DOWN

1. Cutting instrument used by Ammonite slaves in David's reign
2. "Only by _____ cometh contention"
3. "The Lord appeared unto Solomon by _____"
5. Instruments for moving a boat
6. Musical instrument
7. "The Lord hath _____ that which he spake"
8. God
9. "_____ the hart panteth after the water brooks"
10. Can mean "to prevent"; word used 16 times in the Authorized Version
16. "His _____ also shall not wither"
17. One who gathers information about an enemy
19. "The weaned child shall put his hand on the cockatrice' _____"
20. King who died of a foot disease
24. Not to be broken
25. Jacob described his days as "few and _____"
26. Symbol of human vessel of God; two words
27. Sodom's king in Abraham's day
28. Masculine pronoun used first in Genesis 1:5
30. To try
32. Malchus temporarily lost one
34. Type of bird; perhaps a vulture or hawk

	1	2		3		4	5		6		7	8	9		10
11								12							
13					14										
								15	16		17				
18				19		20									
						21					22				
23	24		25		26										
										27					28
29			30			31		32		33		34			
			35												
36		37				38									39
40					41										

ACROSS

41. Not to be used as a means of killing for food

DOWN

36. At Gethsemane it represented Jesus' impending suffering
39. Number of most species saved on the ark

117

ACROSS

1. Untrue; used 64 times in the Authorized Version
5. Ben-ammi's brother
7. King of Assyria
9. Where there isn't one, "the crib is clean"
10. To beg
11. Tola's son
12. His descendants served as Israel's priests
13. Sinful indulgence
16. Shammah's father
18. Used to control a horse
20. False prophetess in Nehemiah's day
22. God promised he would _____ 15 years to Hezekiah's life
24. "After I am waxed _____ shall I have pleasure?"
25. Listed after the snail in Leviticus 11
28. Aram's second son
29. Philistine god
31. "The _____ cometh, when no man can work"
33. Judah's son killed by God
34. "Ye have _____ of patience"
36. "The Lord is my rock, and my _____"
38. "Ye pay tithe of mint and anise and _____"
40. Achan's father
41. Hittites were his descendants
43. Zephaniah predicted Moab would become like this
44. "The plowman shall overtake the _____"

DOWN

1. Protective area for sheep
2. Alternate spelling of a chopping instrument
3. Saul was plagued by an evil one
4. God
5. First created human gender
6. What Jacob did with some idols at Shechem
7. Life's journey
8. He lived 777 years
14. One of the first descriptions of earth
15. "Let us _____ with patience"
17. Jewish month occurring during July and August
19. Can be any object distracting attention from God
21. "Thou anointest my head with _____"
22. Israel called Dan "an _____ in the path"
23. "_____ sinful nation, a people laden with iniquity"
25. "Even the sea _____ . . . give suck to their young ones"
26. Number of sheep lost in the Parable of the Good Shepherd
27. God declares "the _____ from the beginning"
30. Form of "to be"; used 3,002 times in the Authorized Version
32. Horse's neck clothed with this in Job 39:19
35. Denotes individuality; used 50 times in the Authorized Version
36. Ezekiel saw creatures with four of these
37. God never does this

PUZZLE 57

DOWN

39. Of the house of Caleb
43. Greek letter now used as a ratio

ACROSS

1. Her son watched the shadow of the sun move backwards
3. "He that is _____ of spirit exalteth folly"
5. Sea bordering Egypt
7. "_____ still and know that I am God"
8. "In full _____ of faith"
11. Preposition used 14,130 times in the Authorized Version
12. To be located somewhere
13. Old woman who saw Baby Jesus
15. To have ingested; used only three times in the Authorized Version
17. Hammer used by metalworkers
19. Solomon sent 20,000 baths of this to Tyre
20. City so wicked its name is now used to describe perversion
22. Clenched hand
24. Referred to an enormous container of water in Solomon's temple
25. Belief in only one God
29. Can mean "in this manner"

DOWN

1. Between Tammuz and Elul
2. Another word for "animal"
3. Another word for "hast"
4. Young virgin who married David in his old age
6. Chosen by God
8. King of Assyria brought settlers to Samaria from here
9. Separates man from God
10. Decreed that "all the world should be taxed"
12. Reparation for an offense
14. His son led Israel after Moses' death
16. "_____ things work together for good"
18. "_____, now speakest thou plainly"
21. Where seven fat cows ate in Pharaoh's dream
23. Can be part of a verb or a preposition
26. Spike
27. Ezekiel drew the city of Jerusalem on one

ACROSS

30. "_____, O Israel: The Lord our God is one Lord"
32. Cain was one
33. Priest whose descendents returned from exile with Zerubbabel

DOWN

28. God put one on Cain
31. God

ACROSS

1. Nineteenth letter of the Hebrew alphabet
4. To desecrate something holy
7. Twelth letter of the Greek alphabet
8. Joshua hanged the king of this town
9. Indefinite pronoun used 6,875 times in the Authorized Version
10. Instrumental in Timothy's godly upbringing
11. "Thou shalt make them as a fiery _____"
12. Babylonian Baal
15. One of Jonathan's gifts to David
18. "Exalt [wisdom], and she shall _____ thee"
21. "_____ foolish questions, and genealogies"
22. Spelled with a *u* in the Authorized Version; refers to a smell
23. Phanuel's daughter
24. Onesiphorus looked for Paul there

DOWN

1. Arrows stored here
2. Paul was well acquainted with it
3. Opposite of "to miss"
4. She helped many; a deaconess
5. Caused by disobedience
6. Hyphenated title of God meaning "God Almighty"
13. Can mean "Behold!"
14. Egyptian city
16. "He shall set engines of _____ against thy walls"
17. Type of head covering
18. Demanded his inheritance, then wasted it
19. Called a "glass" in the Authorized Version
20. Blood was put on the _____ of Aaron's right hand
25. Wrongdoing
28. "Young lions _____ after their prey"
29. Often used as a musical instrument
31. Symbol of Issachar

ACROSS

26. Seer and prophet whose book is referred to by the chronicler
27. Second one experienced at salvation
30. Egyptian god
33. Negative reply
34. "The lion shall eat straw like the _____"
36. Describes God's patience

DOWN

32. Opposite of "on"; used 502 times in the Authorized Version
35. Potipherah was priest there

ACROSS

1. Joseph accused his brothers of being _____
4. Jesus' name for Peter
7. Word meaning "son"; used as a prefix in Jewish names
8. "Is there no _____ in Gilead?"
9. Ancestral head of a family in Asher
11. "_____ man"; describes life before salvation
13. God views it as murder
15. Animal Solomon imported
17. Judah's third king
18. Exclamation used 18 times in the Authorized Version
20. Jesus did this for our sins
22. Another name for Ra
23. Prophet contemporary with Zechariah
25. "Confidence in an unfaithful man . . . is like a broken _____"
26. "Let God be _____, but every man a liar"
28. Tribe of Arabs

DOWN

2. Represented spiritual truth in Jesus' parable
3. Trees used for idolatrous sacrifices
4. "This is an heinous _____"
5. Writing instrument
6. "Her clothing is _____ and purple"
7. Balsam tree
10. Snake
11. Forty men took one to kill Paul
12. Ehud's had two edges
13. Reuben fought them during Saul's reign
14. Mercenaries from there hired by Ammonites against David
15. Son of Benjamin
16. Pierced when a slave chose lifelong servitude
19. Noah's great-grandson through Ham and Canaan
21. "_____, one born in my house is mine heir"
24. "Benjamin shall ravin as a _____"
25. Barak gathered 10,000 soldiers there

ACROSS

29. Jesus called Herod a
    _____
32. Jesus asked the
    Pharisees if they would
    rescue one on the
    Sabbath
33. Title for Jesus
34. Fibers of flax

DOWN

27. Asa's grandmother
    made one
30. Nehemiah refused an
    invitation to go there
31. Greek *m*

ACROSS

1. Long handled fork used to throw grain in the air
2. Paul rebuked a sorcerer there
5. Water is stored there
7. Gate at the temple; two words
9. Gem setting
10. "_____ thine house in order"; God's message to Hezekiah
11. One who winnows grain
14. To ridicule
15. "_____ was upon the face of the deep"
17. Hanun cut half of this off
19. Jesus is this
21. Plant used as a medicine
22. Male sheep
23. Gallio was the deputy there
26. Galilean fisherman who had his name changed
28. "Ezra had prepared his heart to _____ the law of the Lord"
29. Israel was commanded not to let their children "_____ through the fire to Molech"

DOWN

1. Trenches created by plowing
2. Pharaoh ordered her to kill male children
3. One who works with clay
4. Utensil used in the temple
5. One who follows a false god
6. "_____ not one to another"
7. Saul's great-great-grandfather
8. Article used 36,466 times in the Authorized Version
12. Descendant of Ephraim
13. Indefinite article used 1,660 times in the Authorized Version
15. Waste residue left from smelting
16. Son of Caleb
17. Supports a roof
18. Type of offering
20. God put man in Eden "to _____ it"
24. Was the grandfather of his own children
25. Direction referred to 2,484 times in the Authorized Version

ACROSS

30. Blood was put on Aaron's during his consecration

DOWN

27. "_____ man hath seen God at any time"

ACROSS

6. Sorrowful book
7. David hid in one to get away from Saul
9. One who is humble has this spirit
10. Aided in childbirth
11. Preposition and part of a verb; used 14,112 times in the Authorized Version
13. Ezekiel named them as enemies of Judah
14. Rebelled against Moses
15. God told Elijah to "_____ thyself by the brook Cherith"
18. Piece of flooring in the temple
20. Came home with Ezra after captivity
22. God's is on the sparrow
23. Measure of distance a Jew had to carry a Roman load
24. Father of Hanniel
26. Babylonian-Assyrian god of the sky
29. Awaken
30. _____ places; used for idolatrous worship

DOWN

1. "He becometh poor that dealeth with a _____ hand"
2. Prophet who wrote the longest book in the Bible
3. God's Spirit lifts one against the enemy
4. Hole or cistern
5. Had to be removed from the temple regularly
8. Sacrificed his sons by rebuilding Jericho
9. Copper is one
12. Fluid used in writing
13. Ornament used on the seven-branched lampstand
16. Shuppim's father
17. Sorcerer struck blind
19. Great river
20. Mushi's son
21. "O Lord . . . keep the _____ of my lips"
23. NIV rendering of "fable"
25. "I can _____ all things through Christ"
27. Compass point
28. Exclamation used 38 times in the Authorized Version

PUZZLE 62

1
2
3
4
5
6
7
8
9
10
11
12
13
14
15
16
17
18
19
20
21
22
23
24
25
26
27
28
29
30

ACROSS

1. Zilpah's first son
3. Insulted Noah, his father
5. Peter fell into one
8. To tear
10. Childbirth
11. Pharaoh under Shalmanesar's empire
12. Title for Psalm 119:97-104
14. Asenath's father worked there
15. Third son of Cush
17. Used to cement bricks
18. Abner's grandfather
20. Denotes motion; used 1,479 times in the Authorized Version
21. Jesus told Peter, "_____ my sheep"
23. He was destroyed for making a wrong offering
24. Old Testament book describing the Jew's resettlement after captivity
26. "Be ye kind one _____ another"
27. Used to move goods
28. Benjamite town
29. Dwelling place for those who reject Christ

DOWN

1. Moses commanded that the Law be preached from this mountain
2. City that marked the northern limit of Israel
3. Hebrew letter introducing Psalm 119:33-40
4. Means "tomorrow"; used 103 times in the Authorized Version
5. Process of change in form
6. Town of Asher
7. City built by Cain and named after his son
9. Another word for "hind"
12. Where goods were bought and sold
13. Ram's eldest son
16. God is "slow to _____, and of great kindness"
18. Nabal's widow who married David
19. Sediments found in wine
22. "Depart from evil, and _____ good"
23. Angel of the abyss
25. Disciple of Christ
28. "As an _____ goeth to the slaughter"; an immoral man

ACROSS

30. City whose name was changed to Dan
32. Preposition used 1,536 times in the Authorized Version
33. Abraham's nephew
34. Eliasaph's father
35. Jesus offers new _____

DOWN

29. Greeting
31. Shem's grandson

ACROSS

1. Stones used by warriors
7. Regarding parents' instructions: "_____ them about thy neck"
9. Method used to tear down walls referred to by Ezekiel
11. Capital of Upper Egypt
13. God created every one
16. Canaanite people
19. Story relating a spiritual truth
21. NIV reference to waste of sacrificial animal
23. Solomon strengthened this place
25. Dry stalks of grain
27. One was being taken at Jesus' birth
28. She married her uncle Herod
31. One of five Midianite Kings slain at the command of Moses
33. Free gift of God through Christ
35. Constellation mentioned in Job and Amos

DOWN

1. Jesus used it with dirt to anoint a blind man's eyes
2. Shuppim and Huppim were his sons
3. Moses sent him to spy on Canaan
4. Jephthah fled to this place
5. Through Hosea, God called Israel's leaders "a _____ spread upon Tabor"
6. "_____ with his fathers"; expression referring to death
7. Sent his son to David as an ambassador
8. "If he shall ask an _____, will he offer him a scorpion?"
10. "Caught up . . . to meet the Lord in the _____"
12. Ancestor of Jesus; Nagge's son
14. Adam was the first to lose one
15. Roman appointed ruler in Jesus' day
17. Gather together
18. Gehazi became "white as _____" with Naaman's leprosy
19. Enclosed litter used as transportation in Bible times
20. Zechariah's daughter
22. No one has seen God's
23. Type of club compared to one who "bears false witness"
24. "_____ a black horse"
26. Jesus healed him of palsy through Peter's prayer
28. Storehouse
29. Lot and his daughters lived in one

DOWN

30. Noah saw a great deal of this
32. Fat priest
34. Another name for 11 across

ACROSS

1. Hill near Jerusalem
5. Evil government official left hanging
8. Palsied man healed there
9. Pharaoh whose tomb became famous in modern times
10. Sick
11. Ishmael's mother
13. Pottery fragment important to archaeologists
14. Son of Noah
16. God never does this
19. Name meaning "black"; man from Antioch church
21. Means "beginning"
22. Name Jesus gave to James and John
25. "To this _____ also did I write"
27. Paul wore them
29. God put _____ between the serpent and the woman
31. Land of Cain's wandering
33. Father
35. Night light
36. Masculine pronoun used 9,964 times in the Authorized Version

DOWN

1. Massive wooden door through a city wall
2. Boaz loved her
3. Pestilence similar to mildew
4. Smell
5. Fire is mingled with this in Revelation
6. Sister of Lot who married her uncle Nahor
7. Head of a family that could not prove their Israelite descent
12. Egyptian god
14. Jesus compared himself to one
15. One Mary was from there
17. Generally applied to the Scythians; used symbolically for evil forces
18. Ring used as a seal
20. Type of grain
22. Israelites rebuked here by an angel
23. Jesus is _____ from the dead
24. Killed while trying to steal Philistine cattle
26. Father of Micaiah, a prophet in Ahab's day

1		2		3		4		5		6		7
				8								
9								10				
		11										
12						13						
14		15		16		17						
										18		
19				20		21						
22				23		24			25			
						26						
27		28				29				30		
					31	32		33	34			
35								36				

DOWN

28. City captured by Ben-hadad in return for Asa's gift
30. Measure of time
32. Belonging to
34. "_____ strong and of a good courage"

ACROSS

1. One of Egypt's plagues
4. "Give us this day our _____ bread"
8. Preposition used 14,130 times in the Authorized Version
9. King Hadar ruled there
10. He was unworthy of priestly duties
11. Minor prophet mentioned in apocryphal *Bel and the Dragon*
13. To kill
15. Tended David's camels
17. Handle of a sword or dagger
19. Zaccur's father
20. Symbols of authority
22. Disownment
24. Abraham almost used one on Isaac
27. "Hast thou not . . . curdled me like _____?" Job asked
29. First human dwelling place
31. Two words describing Ehud's choice of members
34. Tells of the reconstruction of the temple

DOWN

1. Often made of bone
2. Midianite prince beheaded
3. Joseph was told his father was _____
5. City captured after Joshua's death
6. One with a skin disease
7. To be "_____ off"; executed
9. Architectural support of which Samson broke two
12. Not omitting any; used 5,483 times in the Authorized Version
14. You; used 3,780 times in the Authorized Version
16. Creeping vine
17. Esther's Hebrew name
18. Costly material
21. Peter saw one come out of heaven
23. Pharaoh accused the Israelites of being _____
25. God sent Jonah there
26. David's eldest brother
28. First letter of the Hebrew alphabet
30. Jacob's daughter
32. Asa had a disease in his

ACROSS

36. Let it be
38. To strike
39. Not idle
40. Appendage on the head of many ungulates, used as a wind instrument

DOWN

33. "Sadducees, which _____ . . . any resurrection"
35. Jewish month
37. "I had _____ rest in my spirit"

ACROSS

1. Title of last section of Psalm 119
2. Direction in which the wise men travelled
5. Thirteenth letter of the Hebrew alphabet
7. Jesus turned water into wine there
8. Ancient country in lower Euphrates/Tigris valley
10. Resin used to make perfume
12. Pauline epistle to believers in a Macedonian city
17. Animal imported by Solomon
19. Valuable tooth material
21. Container used for liquids
22. Jewish month
23. Not to be the center of attention
25. Zechariah saw "a man with a measuring _____"
28. Name for God
29. Evildoer
31. By-product of fire
32. God owns "the _____ upon a thousand hills"
33. He and Levi tricked the Hivites

DOWN

1. Zeba and Zalmunna killed Gideon's brothers there
2. Rahab lived on one
3. Transgression against God
4. Re
5. Target of Peter's sword
6. Persian prince under Ahasuerus
7. Three words describing a method of choosing
9. Liquid measure
11. Part of the mouth
13. "They _____ wait for their own blood"
14. God's tranquility
15. Evil sheepmaster from Maon
16. Storage pool
18. Not fat
20. "Will a man _____ God?"
22. "_____ this power will I give thee"; Satan's promise
23. One bound to serve another
24. Allow
26. We are created in God's
27. Wise man in Solomon's time
30. To consume food

PUZZLE 67

1
2
3
4
5
6
7
8
9
10
11
12
13
14
15
16
17
18
19
20
21
22
23
24
25
26
27
28
29
30
31
32
33

ACROSS

1. Called an "axletree" in the Authorized Version
3. Temporary stopping place
7. Really referred to a lamp
8. Authorized Version spelling of a boring instrument
9. Head of the eunuchs of Babylon
12. Fishing vessel
14. "For _____ us a child is born"
15. "Like a deer stepping into a _____"
16. Paul encouraged Titus to "rebuke with all _____"
20. Head of a priestly family that returned from Babylon
21. Zephaniah's son
23. Weapon of war; symbol of God's anointing on Joshua
26. David's activity before the Ark
29. Binding agreement
30. Plant disease referred to in the NIV

DOWN

1. Gadite soldier
2. City defeated by Joshua
3. Peter found one in a fish
4. Jerahmeel's grandson
5. Jewish leader at Casiphia
6. Dwelling of the nomad
7. A group
10. Chief servant of Abraham
11. Site of a final battle
12. Wild pig mentioned in Psalm 80
13. Leah was Joseph's
15. Mephibosheth's dropped him
17. Part of a verb
18. Delivered Israel from Cushanrishathaim
19. There was no room there
22. Shall be last
24. Highly fragrant plant
25. There is but _____ true God
27. _____ and Magog
28. Thebes

PUZZLE 68

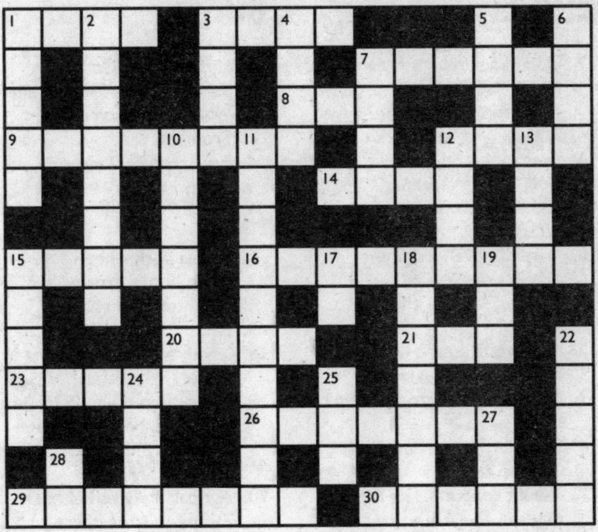
1
2
3
4
5
6
7
8
9
10
11
12
13
14
15
16
17
18
19
20
21
22
23
24
25
26
27
28
29
30

ACROSS

2. Nebuchadnezzar's dream image had a chest and _____ of silver
4. Ruled Egypt in Ahaz's day
6. Aramaic word meaning "why"
8. God "is like a refiner's fire, and like fuller's _____"
10. Male of royal heritage
11. Achish's opinion of David: "_____, ye see the man is mad"
12. Toil; word used 416 times in the Authorized Version
13. Hebrew letter pronounced like h
14. Direction first mentioned in Genesis 2:6
17. Plural pronoun used 1,432 times in the Authorized Version
18. Stephen was _____
21. Jesus was often called this
24. Cutting tool
26. "_____ profane and vain babblings"
27. He made silver shrines to the goddess Diana in Ephesus
29. To put a hole through
31. Samuel's mother
33. God set them in the sky
35. Naomi asked to be called this
39. Moses' father
40. Preposition used 14,130 times in the Authorized Version
41. He walked with Elijah

DOWN

1. Jesus _____ God's Son
2. Solomon imported this animal
3. One sent to scout the Promised Land
4. Paul's companion
5. Town built by Shemed, a Benjamite, in the territory of Dan
6. Sexual wickedness
7. From Judah; married the daughter of a pharaoh
9. Last
15. Jewish festival originating in Esther
16. Preposition used 1,536 times in the Authorized Version
19. Peter prayed and God restored her life
20. Agriculturally useful beast
21. Ruth was from there
22. Can mean "very"
23. Joseph spent time in one
25. Used as a religious curse by Hebrews
27. Edict
28. Samson stayed at the rock of _____
30. Reubenite chief who rebelled with Korah
32. Used to be a description of character as well as a title
34. Beast in Revelation had seven heads and _____ horns
36. Type of tree
38. Sixteenth letter in the Greek alphabet

PUZZLE 69

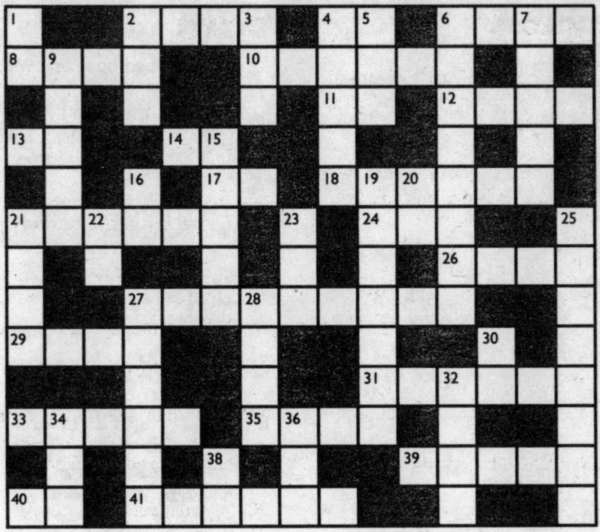

ACROSS

1. Almighty One
3. Pronoun; used 2,681 times in the Authorized Version
6. Rebelled against Abimelech
9. Jewish month
10. "They that _____ upon the Lord shall renew their strength"
11. "The name of the wicked shall _____"
13. "Then shall the lame man _____"
16. Judah's wicked son
17. Another name for Ra
18. Baby Moses was hidden among these; called "flags" in the Authorized Version
19. John saw creatures with "_____ in their tails"
20. Two words; David's place of refuge on the Dead Sea's west coast
22. Early Arab; son of Joktan
24. Tribe that defeated Leshem in order to expand their territory
26. His son, Geber, was a supply officer for Solomon
28. "Like a crane or a _____, so did I chatter"
30. King Hoshea made an alliance with him
31. We are like _____ sheep gone astray
33. Egyptians believed he created all things
34. Was a prisoner, then a ruler, in one day

DOWN

1. Joel described how one was sold for wine
2. Athenian converted by Paul
4. Three words describing one function of the Gibeonites
5. To strike
6. "Let us now _____ even unto Bethlehem"
7. Aromatic plant
8. Fortress near the temple where Paul was taken
12. Psalm 1 compares a righteous man to one
14. "My tongue is the _____ of a ready writer"
15. To utilize; used 35 times in the Authorized Version
19. Proverbs compares an indiscrete woman with gold in a swine's _____
21. Canaanite god of fortune
23. Human sacrifices made to Molech there
25. Prophet who ministered during the reign of Jeroboam II
27. He loved Rebekah
29. Bulbs from these plants used to season along with onions and garlic
32. Gideon's promise: "I will _____ your flesh with . . . thorns"

ACROSS

35. Old ones were used by the Gibeonites
36. One who worked with leather; Peter stayed with such a person

ACROSS

5. Jesus called him Satan once
7. Was more concerned with entertaining Jesus than listening to him
10. Name for God
11. Capital of King Hadar of Edom
12. Used to row a boat
13. Trial allowed by God to mature faith
14. His mother hid him
16. One of the Levite musicians entering Jerusalem with the Ark
17. Her faith was commended by Paul
19. He lost his sight for three days but found Christ
22. Persian ruler who allowed the Jews to rebuild the temple
25. "Of the tree of the knowledge of good and evil, thou shalt not _____"
28. Ten were sent upon Egypt
30. Animal mentioned in Revelation
32. One of Rehoboam's sons

DOWN

1. Used to make an ointment that healed a blind man
2. "The elements shall _____ with fervent heat"
3. Egyptian god
4. He once led Israel into idolatry
6. "Our iniquities _____ against us"
7. "I _____ on the work of thy hands"
8. Jesus' body lay in a borrowed one
9. Exclamation used in one verse of Job
11. "Blessed are the _____ in spirit"
15. Isaiah mentioned such a person in conjunction with astrology
18. Greek m
20. Blood-sucking creature used in ancient medicine
21. Indefinite pronoun used 6,875 times in the Authorized Version
23. Pharaoh gave Joseph his
24. Dipped in vinegar and offered to Jesus
26. "Your country is desolate . . . _____ overthrown by strangers"

146

ACROSS

33. Of Absalom it was said, "There was _____ blemish in him"
34. Hosea used the term to refer to idolatrous priests

DOWN

27. Son of Abraham by Keturah
29. Expression of agreement
31. Cutting tool

ACROSS

1. Deaconess highly recommended by Paul/Authorized Version spelling
4. Corrupt, bad
6. Egyptian mother of Ishmael
8. He had to marry his brother's widow
9. Ninth of 13 descendants of Joktan
12. "_____, I am with you always"
14. Danger to Paul's ship as a storm began
16. "I have nourished and brought _____ children"
17. Musician at the dedication of Jerusalem's wall
18. David cut off the _____ of Saul's robe
20. Color symbolizing royalty and obtained from sea animals
21. Prince of the tribe of Asher who helped divide Canaan
23. Animal that ate Jezebel
24. "Is there any taste in the white of an _____?"

DOWN

1. To tell about; used 23 times in the Authorized Version
2. Mountain opposite Gerizim
3. Eighth of the minor prophets
4. Onan's brother
5. "An _____ soul shall suffer hunger"
7. Son of Midian and grandson of Abraham
10. Started a Benjamite clan
11. Spotted animal that once lived in Palestine
13. Brings death
14. Places where stone is cut
15. "Be careful for _____"
18. "The love of God is _____ abroad in our hearts by the Holy Ghost"
19. Rachel stole Laban's _____
20. "God shall wipe away all tears . . . neither shall there be any more _____"
22. Part of the high priest's breastplate by which he determined the will of God

ACROSS

25. God breathed into Adam's _____ the breath of life
26. First person singular pronoun used 4,402 times in the Authorized Version

ACROSS

1. Article of furniture Ezekiel mentions as made of ivory
3. Having to do with Satan's forces
7. Ruled Judah, then all of Israel
10. First month of year in modern Judaism
11. The husband of the woman who was turned into a pillar of salt
12. Jesus is _____
13. Can move mountains
16. Capital of a world empire in Jesus' day
17. Paul used this organ as an example of the Christian's unique talents
18. Jesus turned water into this
19. She lived in Jericho
20. "Thou art _____, O Lord"
21. Roman emperor who probably had Paul executed
22. We are told to turn the other one
23. What Haman planned to do to Mordecai

DOWN

1. "Take up thy _____, and walk"
2. Three words; what Christians are
3. Daniel went into the lions'
4. Means "anointed one"
5. Joshua's father
6. "Can ye drink of the _____ that I drink of?"
8. In time past; used 13 times in the Authorized Version
9. "I delight to _____ thy will"
12. "I delight in the _____ of God after the inward man"
13. Two words; one was used sent to David as he returned to Jerusalem
14. Language of the Jews
15. Israelite slaves made these for the Egyptians
24. Jair's 30 sons rode on 30 "_____ colts"
26. "If we say that we have fellowship with him, and walk in darkness, we _____"
27. Maker of honey

PUZZLE 73

ACROSS

25. "_____ is joy to him that is destitute of wisdom"
28. "The Lord _____ our refuge and strength"
29. What you owe another
30. Fortified city of Naphtali

ACROSS

2. Naomi's daughter-in-law
6. Noah saw a great one
9. What Joseph could not find
10. Abraham camped between this city and Bethel when he arrived in Canaan
12. One of Joktan's 13 sons
13. One led Samson to the pillars he pulled down
14. John "saw the souls of them that were beheaded for the _____ of Jesus"
16. "_____, an horror of great darkness fell"
17. Benjamite city
18. Landmark on the eastern border of the Promised Land
19. Nehemiah was one to Artaxerxes
21. Condition of Gideon's fleece
22. Twelfth letter of the Greek alphabet
23. Long term for lying
26. Adam was the first one

DOWN

1. "Henceforth there is laid up for me a _____ of righteousness"
2. Sign of a future event
3. Small green vegetables
4. Fifth letter of the Hebrew alphabet
5. One who owes
6. "Be ye of me, even as I also am of Christ"
7. Used to fuel lamps
8. Arabian people descended directly from Noah
11. Name appearing 2,550 times in the Authorized Version, counting possessives, which means "He strives with God"
15. Last letter of the Hebrew alphabet
18. Reconciliation of God and man through the death of Christ
19. Spice
20. Only flying mammal; an unclean food
24. Boring instrument
25. He beat his donkey
27. God meets all of ours

PUZZLE 74

ACROSS

29. Father of Eliasaph whose name means "belonging to God"
31. "Cease from _____, and forsake wrath"
32. To reach a destination
34. Another name for Obadiah, the son of Shemaiah
35. Book of early church history
36. Intercessor

DOWN

28. Another name for Simon
30. Aramaic word for *father*
31. Third king of Judah
33. "A _____ is for the back of him that is void of understanding"

ACROSS

3. Portion of Egypt in which the Israelites lived
7. Grow alongside rivers and in standing waters
9. A fever (as malaria)
10. One doesn't fall without God knowing it
13. May have been Moab's capital
14. Office in the church
16. Belonging to him; used 7,554 times in the Authorized Version
17. Reaping tools
18. Egyptian king
19. "Charity" is an old word for this
20. Type of gem
24. Not near; used 172 times in the Authorized Version
25. Shot from a bow
27. Master of a household
28. "Be ye not unequally _____ together with unbelievers"

DOWN

1. Sediment in the bottom of wine
2. Place on the southern border of Judah
4. Bread placed before God
5. One of David's sons born in Jerusalem
6. "All we like _____ have gone astray"
8. People in Shinar baked these to make a tower
11. Jesus celebrated it the night before his death
12. Hebrew name for the grave, or hell
15. "As the hart panteth after the water brooks, _____ panteth my soul after thee, O God"
18. "Where _____ abounded, grace did much more abound"
20. Brother of Miriam
21. Symbol of strength
22. Jesus arose on the _____ day
23. Came when Jesus spoke to the storm
24. Type of tree that withered at Jesus' rebuke
26. "I am the _____, the truth, and the life"

154

PUZZLE 75

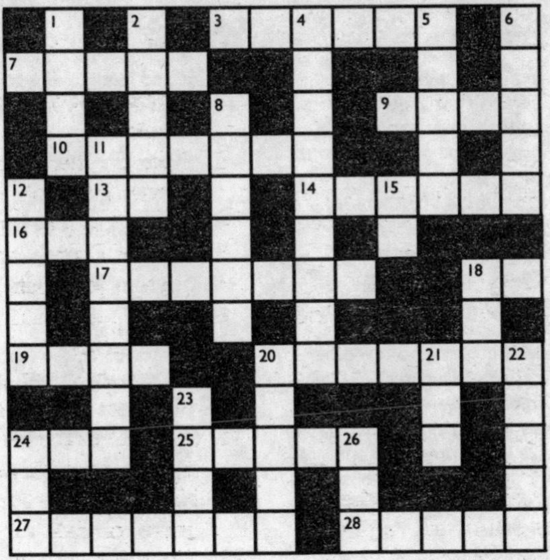

ACROSS

1. Land of the pyramid
6. God and two angels appeared to Abraham as three _____
8. Hoshea made an alliance with him
9. Name of hill in Athens where Paul spoke
10. Moabite region or city
11. God told Moses, "I _____"
13. In the same way
14. Young goat
15. Jewish queen who saved her race from slaughter
17. Listening organ
20. Also known as Dorcas
21. Jesus is the promised one
24. Another word for white
25. Sixteenth letter of the Greek alphabet
26. Elijah told to do so by an angel
28. Month between Tammuz and Elul
29. Phoenician port south of Sidon
32. Omega
34. Benjamite town
35. Only God is this
37. Female deer
38. To test
39. Means "adversary"

DOWN

1. Lot and family were told, "_____ for thy life; look not behind"
2. "_____ to now, ye rich men"
3. "_____ I leave with you"
4. Town in Edom; also Shobal's son
5. First of five kings in Judah known for their righteousness
6. Four words describing the sign of allegiance to the Antichrist
7. Onan's brother
12. God's people made their hearts like this hard stone
16. Teacher
18. Twentieth letter of the Hebrew alphabet
19. Satan "is a _____, and the father of it"
21. John the Baptist's was locusts and wild honey
22. "For as his name is, _____ is he"
23. "A fire gone out of Heshbon . . . hath consumed _____ of Moab"
27. Among the animals, "there was not _____ an help meet" for Adam
30. Seventeenth letter of the Greek alphabet
31. Language in which the New Testament was written
33. "If we _____ him, he also will _____ us"
35. Jesus is God's only begotten _____
36. "_____, a Lamb stood on the mount Sion"

ACROSS

2. One who performs magic and trickery; was to be stoned
6. Jehu's grandfather
7. Seasoning
9. Jesus was called "Rabbi," or _____
10. Exclamation
11. Egyptian god
13. Witchcraft
14. Another word for "knob"
17. Belonging to him; used 7,554 times in the Authorized Version
19. Given to the poor
21. One who studied astronomy
24. Where the star was seen
25. "A good name is rather to be _____ than great riches"
26. Egyptian city
27. "Let their table be made a snare, and a _____"
28. City that could not be conquered until Achan confessed his sin

DOWN

1. Worker in metal at one time not found in Israel
2. "Rebellion is as the sin of _____"
3. Grandfather of Oholibamah, Esau's wife
4. Tool of the shepherd
5. Was one of the two good spies
6. "They sacrificed unto devils . . . to _____ gods"
8. Name meaning watcher
12. "Who can utter the mighty _____ of the Lord?"
13. Onesimus was one
14. What Israel demanded of Samuel
15. Exclamation used for the first time in Genesis 18:30
16. Sixteenth letter of the Greek alphabet
18. "Who is this King of glory? The Lord _____ and mighty"
20. King of Moab in the days of Ahab
22. Used to make healing ointments
23. She saw Baby Jesus at the temple

ACROSS

2. "Thou shalt not suffer a _____ to live"
7. "_____ of the sword"
8. "We have this treasure in earthen _____"
9. One who saw the heavenly host
10. Joab stabbed Absalom with this weapon
12. Can mean "like"
13. Part of Peter's name
16. Judas did this to himself
19. Jephthah fled there
20. Eating vessel
21. He washed his hands before Jesus
24. "Let us draw near . . . in full _____ of faith"
26. "_____ your hands, all ye people"
27. Twelfth letter of the Greek alphabet
28. Book of sorrow

DOWN

1. God promised he would send one
2. Crying
3. Heavenly being
4. "If ye have faith as a grain of mustard _____"
5. Called a "girdle" in the Authorized Version
6. Gathered from the altar
11. Bustling excitement
14. Older form of the name "Jesus"
15. What the seven skinny cows did to the seven fat cows
17. One of David's might men
18. Depart from life; word used 316 times in the Authorized Version
20. Sin was one
22. Another word for the pupil
23. Evil spirit
25. Simeon took Baby Jesus "up in his _____"

PUZZLE 78

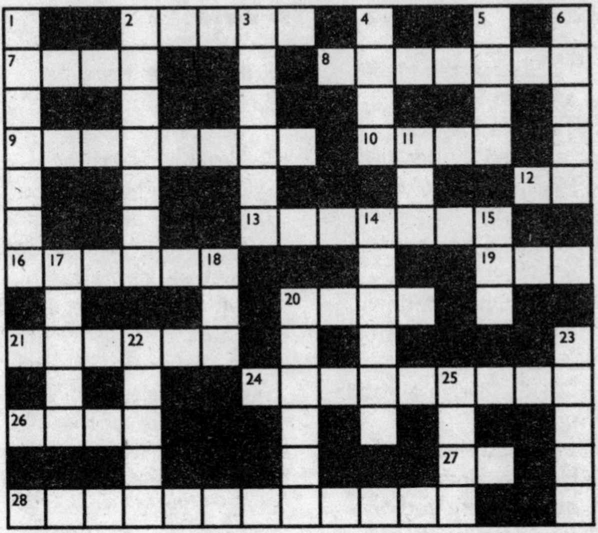

ACROSS

1. "_____ of the Medes and the Persians"
3. Town in Naphtali captured by Ben-hadad
4. Weapons used to hurl stones
9. Where a horse is kept; Solomon had 4,000
10. "Thou shalt lie down, and thy sleep shall be _____"
13. David "died in a good old _____"
15. Twentieth letter of the Hebrew alphabet
17. Book whose author may have been Paul
19. He was "a Pharisee, the son of a Pharisee"
20. Egyptian king
21. Spiritual renewal or revival
23. Jesus said it "bloweth where it listeth"
24. Means "messenger"
27. Wafer used to dip food from a common platter
30. "For unto _____ a child is born"
31. Moses and his family stayed in one

DOWN

1. Improper desire
2. "Fair _____ cometh out of the north"
3. "Love worketh no _____ to his neighbour"
5. His uncle became the father of many nations
6. "Let us draw _____ with a true heart in full assurance of faith"
7. To view; used 591 times in the Authorized Version
8. Fifth letter of the Hebrew alphabet
11. "_____ and rumours of _____"
12. Time when Christ's resurrection is celebrated
14. "These sayings are faithful and _____"
16. "He that uttereth a _____, is a fool"
18. Grain
19. Cooking vessel
20. Planters
21. Body of water separated by God; two words
22. Minor prophet who was a fruit picker
25. "Every word of God is _____"

ACROSS

32. Allow
33. Where Moses spoke with God
34. Plant mentioned for the last time in Scripture in Revelation 22:14

DOWN

26. Old word for you; used 3,510 times in the Authorized Version
28. Sixteenth letter of the Greek alphabet
29. Industrious insect commended in Proverbs

ACROSS

3. Solomon imported this animal
6. He betrayed Christ
9. Command to do something; word used 1,566 times in the Authorized Version
11. God
12. Greek p
13. He bought Joseph
15. King of Bashan
16. Number mentioned 1,898 times in the Authorized Version
17. Relatives
18. "I _____"; one of Jesus' statements from the cross
20. "Let _____ your heart be troubled"
21. Abraham was called the _____ of God
23. "Mine _____ is as nothing before thee"
25. Paul wrote numerous epistles there
27. Egyptian goddess
28. Great number of people
30. Animal that licked Lazarus's sores
32. Animal David killed
33. He was a tax collector
34. Sometimes used to name a false god
36. Word for "you" used 3,780 times in the Authorized Version
38. Samson's hair was woven into one
41. A descendant of Manasseh
42. Waste

DOWN

1. "The joints of thy _____ are like jewels"
2. To be somewhere
4. Is believed to have been crucified upside down
5. Priest who raised Samuel, but was cursed by God
6. The beloved
7. "My God will enlighten my _____"
8. "Thee have I _____ righteous before me," God told Noah
9. "Christ . . . offered himself without _____ to God"
10. "_____ to do well; seek judgment"
13. Gate in Jerusalem wall; two words
14. Egyptian city
19. Can mean "in this manner"
21. Used to separate grain from chaff
22. Another name for the 10th plague
23. Often made of rough stones
24. "Incline thine _____ unto my sayings"
26. Benjamite city
29. Joktan's son
30. To inhabit or stay in a place
31. Part of Great Commission
32. False God worshipped by Israel
33. Moses was this
35. Jesus' father
37. Judah's son
39. Greek m
40. He had an iron bed

PUZZLE 80

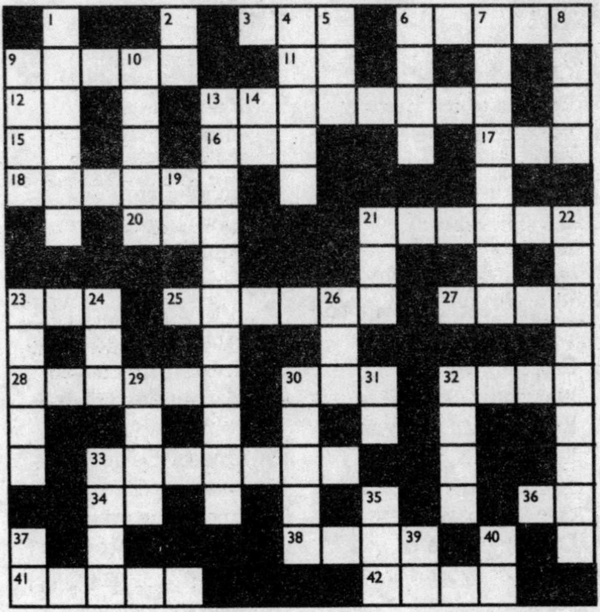

ACROSS

1. Old word for "broom"
4. Lysanius ruled there
8. "The _____ he hath sent empty away"
10. Jehoiakim used one to cut up Jeremiah's message
11. Unable to have children
12. "Their feet are swift to _____ blood"
14. Prophet whom Naaman came to see
16. Represented the gospel in a parable
17. "In process of _____ it came to pass"
19. Dwelling place of evil
21. Another word for "idol"
24. David put the Ark on one
27. Caleb's nephew who judged Israel
28. Plural personal pronoun used 1,772 times in the Authorized Version

DOWN

2. Father of Hophni and Phinehas
3. Myself
5. To send away as punishment
6. One who does evil
7. Adam's companion
8. Type of crime
9. Animals related to rabbits; unclean food
10. Books of Moses
13. Made riding more comfortable
15. One of David's sons
18. Used to ask a question
20. Another name for Iri
22. Agricultural tool
23. "Behold, I make all things _____"
25. Means "to be"; used 845 times in the Authorized Version
26. Part of infinitive

ACROSS

1. Melchizedek was king and priest there
4. "_____ cometh, when no man can work"
6. Aramaic word for "father"
7. Jesus' meal before his arrest is known as the Last _____
8. Fifth king of the northern kingdom
11. One of five Midianite kings killed at Moses' command
12. Jewish month
13. "_____ God, _____ God, why hast thou forsaken me?"
14. Jacob's fifth son
16. Son of Pethuel who authored the second book of the Minor Prophets
17. Canaanite royal city to which Solomon later assigned forced labor
18. Egyptian king
19. Seventh book of the minor prophets
21. Eve was made from one

DOWN

1. Portion of grain left in the field
2. "The lot is cast into the _____"
3. To wed
4. Jesus grew up there
5. He helped hold up Moses' hands during battle
9. Insane
10. No room for Jesus' family there
15. Town in Judah near Edom
16. Loyal friend
17. Second Gospel
18. Second church addressed in Revelation
20. To repay for evil
22. David left 200 of his weaker men there
23. To join together
25. Belonging to
28. Seventeenth letter of the Hebrew alphabet

ACROSS

24. Number of spies sent to Jericho
26. Herb
27. Opposite of "in"; used 2,696 times in the Authorized Version
28. Describes hunger
29. Large-scale conflict
30. "I will sing praise to thy _____"

ACROSS

1. Egyptian god
3. Mixed with fire in the seventh plague
7. Jesus attended a wedding there and performed his first miracle
8. Heavenly messengers
9. Indefinite pronoun used 6,875 times in the Authorized Version
10. Jacob saw one in a dream
14. Wafer for dipping
15. Jacob endured this at night when working for Laban
16. Sarah's original name
17. Article used 36,466 times in the Authorized Version
18. Modern word for ceremonies for the dead
20. Discomfort relieved by scratching
22. Giants
24. Jesus said to offer this to be hit
25. Large protective door to a city
26. Ham's grandson

DOWN

2. To carry out
3. Seventh plague of Egypt
4. Put to rest
5. Man mentioned in Proverbs
6. King mentioned in Ezra
11. "By the word of thy lips I have kept me from the paths of the _____"
12. What we give to God beyond our tithes
13. One of five Jesus blessed to feed thousands
14. "_____ on my right hand, until I make thine enemies thy footstool"
19. Israelites complained about missing this food from Egypt
21. Samson's hair was never supposed to be _____
23. "Thou rulest the raging of the _____"

ACROSS

1. Paul described one in his flesh
4. "Thy rod and thy _____ they comfort me"
8. Exclamation
9. She was adopted by Mordecai; her Jewish name was Hadassah
12. Not near
13. Describes the room where the Holy Spirit baptized believers
15. "O Lord, _____ mine iniquity"
16. Benjamite of Bela's family
18. Elderly members of a community
20. Source of water
22. He was the father of the Moabites and Ammonites
23. Indefinite article used 1,660 times in the Authorized Version
24. Jair's burial place
26. Hatred
29. Nod was _____ of Eden
30. Herod had John's amputated
31. Congregate

DOWN

1. Definite article used 36,466 times in the Authorized Version
2. Prophet whose unfaithful wife symbolized Israel's backsliding
3. Another name for Noah
5. To ensnare
6. "The _____ of the Lord is the beginning of knowledge"
7. One's share
10. Solomon's Edomite adversary
11. Participate in a race
14. Esau's Hittite father-in-law
15. Father of a clan in Issachar
16. One of David's warriors; an Ithrite
17. "_____ by might, nor by power, but by my spirit"
19. First book of the Bible
20. Jerusalem was called this in 2 Samuel 5
21. Paul's young friend
25. Wanderer
27. Tiny amount of money
28. "They shall _____ as lions' whelps"

ACROSS

6. Jesus' return from the dead
9. Donkey
10. High priest after Aaron's death
11. Christ acts as ours
14. Two words; oasis where David hid from Saul
15. Musical instrument used to announce judgment in Revelation
19. Son of Peleg who lived 239 years
20. "By sorrow of the heart the spirit is ____"
23. David's mighty man from Gad
25. Satan's character
26. Jewish court that tried Jesus

DOWN

1. Stopped
2. Spiritual condition of church in Laodicea
3. "The truth shall make you ____"
4. Satan is one
5. Type of dish in the temple
7. Helah's son
8. Seventy were at Elim
12. Christ promised to do this
13. By-product of the hen
16. Jacob's eldest son
17. Second plague
18. Fifth letter of the Hebrew alphabet
21. "Taste and ____ that the Lord is good"
22. Jesus raised a widow's son there
24. Another name for Noah

PUZZLE 85

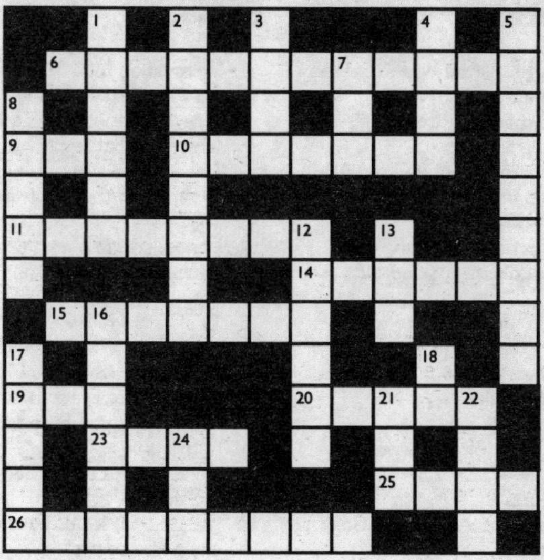

ACROSS

1. They attacked weak Israelites soon after the Exodus
6. Listed as both Benjamin's son and grandson
8. Masculine pronoun used 9,964 times in the Authorized Version
9. God promised Abraham he would die in a "good old _____"
10. Letter from Paul to a man ministering on Crete
12. "We . . . shall . . . meet the Lord in the _____"
13. "_____ of the sword"
15. "Sons of _____; refers to the Hittites
16. Important verb in the Golden Rule
17. Absalom chose Hushai's advice over this man's
21. "As a jewel of gold in a swine's _____"
23. Form of "to be" used 845 times in the Authorized Version
25. Zipporah's father-in-law
26. "God _____ over the heathen: God sitteth upon the throne of his holiness"
27. Jephthah fled there
28. Ruth's father-in-law
31. _____ of the Chaldees
32. Old word for sneezes found in Job 41
33. "The Lord _____ my shepherd"

DOWN

1. Exclamation used 10 times in the Authorized Version
2. Valley mentioned by Zechariah where the Battle of Armageddon will occur
3. Exclamation used to emphasize a fact
4. Her sons were Zimran, Jokshan, Medan, Midian, Ishbak, and Shuah
5. Title at Psalm 119:65
6. He wrote, "I was envious at the foolish, when I saw the prosperity of the wicked"
7. Nebuchadnezzar built a statue in this plain
11. What Jesus caused the blind to do
14. "_____ to, let us build us a city and a tower"
15. One of the five kings who fought Joshua together
17. Preposition used 1,536 times in the Authorized Version
18. Jezebel's father-in-law
19. Antiochus Epiphanes named this city Epiphaneia after himself
20. Hyphenated name for the town in which Mephibosheth lived
21. Wisdom "uttereth her voice in the _____"
22. Elihu was just dying to share his
24. One of several attached to the hem of the high priest's robe
25. Exclamation used 18 times in the Authorized Version

DOWN

29. Means "before"; used 10 times in the Authorized Version
30. His last descendant to be a priest was Abiathar
31. Plural personal pronoun used 1,432 times in the Authorized Version

ACROSS

1. Enemy of the believer
3. Sealing material
5. Partially digested food important in Mosaic Law
6. Led the Israelites by day; _____ _____ a _____
10. Solemn oath
12. To speak; word used 1,056 times in the Authorized Version
13. "_____ you this day whom ye will serve"
15. Common mode of transportation in Bible times
17. One of Daniel's friends
18. Not high; word used 46 times in the Authorized Version
19. To "sod" means to _____
20. Toil
21. Naomi gave herself this name
22. All the children of Israel are named in this book

DOWN

2. Used to cover the roof of a house
3. Number used 808 times in the Authorized Version
4. What Peter's name meant
5. Roman instrument of cruel death used on Christ
6. Another name for tar
7. John described his vision in this book
8. One of six in which God created the universe
9. "I count all things but _____"
11. First person plural pronoun
14. High priest in Joiakim's day
15. Married Jezebel
16. Another word for "parable"
18. Crippled
19. Judas had this

PUZZLE 87

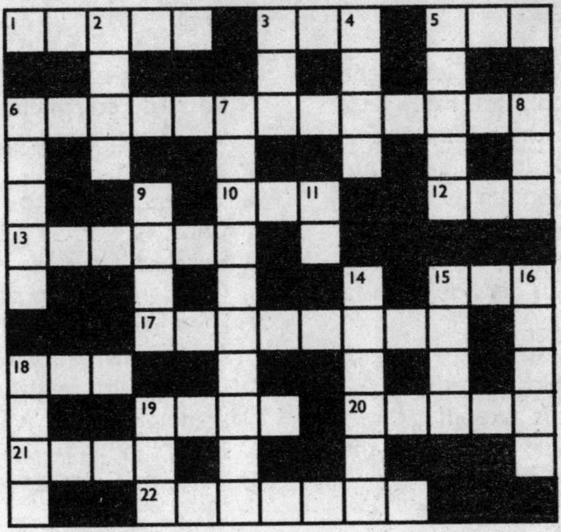

ACROSS

2. Two New Testament books are Paul's letters to these Christians
7. "Be it _____ from me"
8. Hadoram, Uzal, and Diklah were in his family
10. Jesus did not get a fair one
12. "Great peace have they which love thy _____"
14. Jesus asked if a camel could go through the eye of one
16. Which person?
17. Often called a ship
18. Peter found money in one's mouth
20. Egyptian king
21. Pauline epistle
22. Jesus is God's
23. Used to move a boat
24. For fear that
27. Word for "you"; used 3,780 times in the Authorized Version
28. Better to do this than to offer a sacrifice

DOWN

1. Belonging to
2. Reward Peter mentions in I Peter; three words
3. Sick
4. Soldiers did this to Christ
5. Hezekiah's mother
6. God's free gift to man
9. How long one has lived
11. Another name for Ra
12. Dealing with sexual immorality
13. Angel's job
15. Insect that plagued Egypt
19. Adversary
21. To mature
25. Can indicate a destination
26. First person singular pronoun used 4,402 times in the Authorized Version

ACROSS

4. Fifth letter of the Hebrew alphabet
5. Donkey
7. Another name for Jacob
10. Realm of the birds
11. Mother of Jesus
12. Samson slaughtered the Philistines "_____ and thigh"
14. Indefinite article used 1,660 times in the Authorized Version
15. Action of the Magi
16. Another name for Matthew
18. "The _____ of the Lord is upon them that fear him"
19. Always
20. Name of the world's Savior; two words
26. A weed of grainfields
27. God's name; two words
28. Humanity began there
29. Jacob's true love
30. Indefinite pronoun used 6,875 times in the Authorized Version

DOWN

1. Archangel
2. Snare
3. Ruler who executed John the Baptist
4. Noah's disrespectful son
6. Body's natural covering
8. Israel's second military engagement in Canaan
9. "_____ ye the Lord"
13. To talk to God
14. Two drove Lot and his family from Sodom
15. Philistine king who temporarily took Sarah as wife
17. Name for God
21. He aided in returning the Ark
22. Pack animal with large capacity for drink
23. Jordan, Nile—two famous biblical examples of one
24. Satan always tries to do this
25. Guided the wise men to Jesus

PUZZLE 89

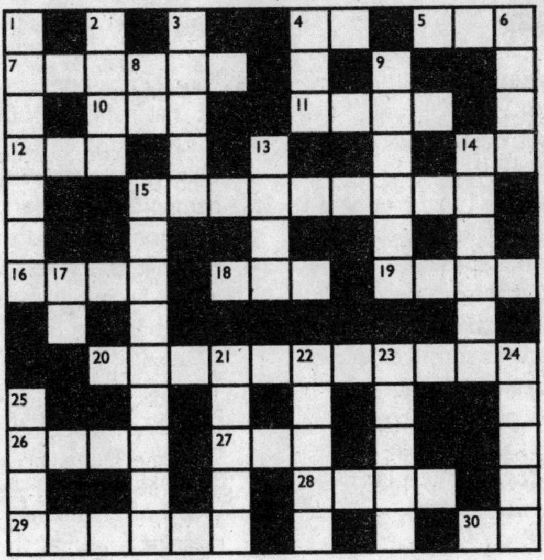

ACROSS

1. Babies are the "fruit of the _____"
5. Jesus raised a widow's son there
8. Benaiah fought using a staff against an _____ with a spear
10. Material from which Sisera's chariots were made
12. Merari's son; founder of a Levitical family
15. Site of Jesus' arrest
18. "_____, children are an heritage of the Lord"
19. Zaccur's father
20. You
21. Plant sown by an enemy in Jesus' parable
22. Held Moses' hands with Aaron
24. To look upon
26. Egyptian pharaoh
27. Wilderness
28. Another word for "since"
31. David's worship when the Ark was brought to Jerusalem
32. Peleg's son
33. Tempting
34. Possessive pronoun used 5,346 times in the Authorized Version

DOWN

1. "Surely . . . the _____ of the nose bringeth forth blood"
2. Quality of possessing compassion or mercy
3. Solomon imported them
4. He built the gallows on which he hung
6. Job sat among this material
7. Thebes
9. His son led Israel after Moses' death
11. Giant king
13. Word of unknown meaning found at the end of phrases in Psalms
14. Roman province Paul referred to as a boundary of his ministry
16. Old word for lame
17. Elpaal's oldest son
23. First person plural pronoun used 1,432 times in the Authorized Version
25. Wilderness west of Edom
26. Plain where the tower of Babel was begun
29. Peter prayed for this paralytic

ACROSS

36. Place of rest for travelers
37. "A wise son _____ his father's instruction"
39. Metaphor for Christians
40. Council that met on Mars Hill

DOWN

30. Laban was Jacob's
31. Ruler who was tricked into putting Daniel in the lions' den
35. "At Tehaphnehes . . . I shall break . . . the _____ of Egypt"
38. Verb used 3,002 times in the Authorized Version

ACROSS

1. Ship that saved the human race
2. Greek philosophical group which pursued pleasure
7. Common rodent; forbidden food
9. Another name for Tiglath-Pileser III
10. "The fear of the Lord is to _____ evil"
11. "As a jewel of gold in a swine's _____"
12. It isn't "satisfied with seeing"
13. Diseased outcast
15. "Lest thou _____ thy foot against a stone"
17. Appointed by David to work for Mephibosheth
19. Joseph's was dipped in animal blood
22. He was healed of leprosy when he washed in the Jordan
25. Condition of the Gibeonites bread
26. Egyptian god
27. Denotes a choice; used 1,015 times in the Authorized Version

DOWN

1. Confrontation between God and Satan in Revelation
2. Without end
3. "_____ in me a clean heart, O God"
4. Egyptian city built by the Israelites
5. Combined with *omega*, it signifies completeness
6. Eastern extremity of Crete
8. Abraham's homeland
10. Aram's second son
14. Used as an example of whiteness
16. Border of a garment
17. Paul asked that he be sent to him with Apollos
18. Sennacherib's sons escaped there after murdering him
19. To change milk to cheese
20. "Why make ye this _____, and weep?"
21. Another name for Tyre
23. Twelve psalms are credited to him
24. Town or region in Moab

ACROSS

28. One of his three sons saw him naked and drunk
29. How the first recorded Christian martyr was killed
31. Wine sediment
33. Word Jesus spoke when healing a deaf and dumb man

DOWN

28. New Testament name for Noah
30. Exclamation used 18 times in the Authorized Version
32. Judah's evil son

ACROSS

1. Paul told the Philippians his troubles were for the "_____ of the gospel"
9. Exclamation used 18 times in the Authorized Version
10. Named with Argob
11. Members of a heretical group in the church at Pergamos
15. Corn grows on one
18. "Godliness with contentment is great _____"
19. Some believe it was the capital of Moab
20. Peter started to do this after walking on water
23. "_____ shall we ever be with the Lord"
24. Redeemed sinners
26. "Forgive, if ye have _____ against any"
28. To be; used 845 times in the Authorized Version
29. Jewish month after Tammuz
30. Author of Proverbs 30
32. Name common in the tribe of Benjamin
33. "A wrathful man stirreth up _____"
36. Noble Hittite; Ephron's father
37. What the Good Shepherd does to the soul
38. Young man; used 33 times in the Authorized Version

DOWN

1. Sins of sexual immorality
2. Egyptian god
3. "Their _____ is an open sepulchre"
4. "With thee will I _____ my covenant"
5. Leah was Joseph's
6. First baby ever born
7. Onan's brother
8. "He shall _____ me up upon a rock"
12. "Serve the Lord thy God with _____ thy heart"
13. "Before the throne there was a _____ of glass like unto crystal"
14. Type of marking on some of Jacob's livestock
16. In the same way
17. To bind something requires its use
21. Sacrificial animal supplied in the place of Isaac
22. Paul said a bishop must be "a _____ of hospitality"
24. Means "hosts"; the Lord of _____
25. Surname of Simeon, leader at church in Antioch
27. One was fixed between the good and evil dead
30. Saul disobeyed God and spared this king
31. _____ of the Chaldees
34. Blood was put there when priests were consecrated
35. To sin

PUZZLE 92

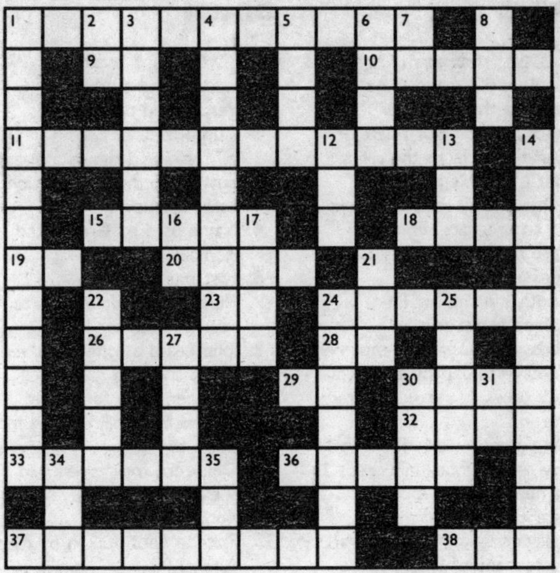

ACROSS

1. "_____ thou at my right hand, until I make thine enemies thy footstool"
3. Also used as "Eloi"; part of Christ's cry from the cross
5. Last of Israel's judges
9. What enemy soldiers would do to pregnant women
10. Verb used 1,331 times in the Authorized Version
11. Another name for Ra
12. Caleb's eldest son
14. Birds and snakes both start here
15. To have the ability to; used 229 times in the Authorized Version
16. King mentioned in Proverbs 31
18. Tower mentioned in Genesis 35
19. Samuel set up a monument near this rock
20. Peleg's son and fifth-generation descendant of Shem
22. Name meaning "watching"
23. "The Lord is not slack concerning his promise, as some men count _____"
27. "I _____ in Sion a chief corner stone"
28. Can mean "proper or fitting"
29. "God . . . breathed _____ his nostrils the breath of life"
31. Type of tree Hosea mentions
32. Strike
33. Second letter in the Greek alphabet
35. "My soul is among lions. . . . They have prepared a _____ for my steps"
36. Town of priests slaughtered by Saul

DOWN

1. "Unleavened bread of _____ and truth"
2. Peace; used once in the Authorized Version
3. NIV refers to this as a disease, but the Authorized Version uses "lunatick"
4. Name used by Greeks and Romans for Edom
6. First murder victim
7. His brother didn't want to raise children for him
8. John heard a song in heaven "no man could _____"
13. Another word for scarlet
17. Abraham's family moved from there to Haran
19. Old word for "appears to be"
21. Shelah's third son
24. Knop
25. Place in Edom taken by King Ahaziah
26. Another name for Shem
30. Name of mountain from which Moses viewed the Promised Land
32. Female chicken
34. Another word for "to spy"
35. God's is not to be used lightly
36. All humanity is descended through this man
39. "Fowls of the _____"
41. Twelfth letter of the Greek alphabet
42. First person pronoun used 4,402 in the Authorized Version

ACROSS

37. "Is _____ sick among you?
    let him call for the elders"
38. "Swear not . . . by any other
    _____"
40. Israel burned this town after
    Achan's death
42. Belonging to me; used 5,346
    times in the Authorized
    Version
43. City in ancient Babylonia;
    second city founded by
    Nimrod
44. Imposed "gift" from one
    country to another

ACROSS

1. Old name for a person from Bethlehem
7. Town on Asher's southern boundary
8. Another word for "tried"
11. To be somewhere; used 1,536 times in the Authorized Version
12. Prophet from Shiloh who predicted Jeroboam would rule 10 tribes
13. Elah's commander who became king
14. Without discipline
17. Fifth letter in the Hebrew alphabet
18. One was caused in Ephesus by Demetrius
20. Town in Benjamin
21. Old word for "you"; used 3,510 times in the Authorized Version
23. Satan is one
25. Indicates a choice; used 1,015 times in the Authorized Version
26. Judah's second son who was killed by God
28. Isaac's second well
30. Shortest of the Gospels
31. "_____ still, and know that I am God"
32. Will not be present in the new earth
34. Revelation describes one with stones weighing more than 100 pounds
36. Donkey
37. Phoenician port south of Sidon
38. Can refer to personal concerns

DOWN

2. Cooking container
3. Process of making something right
4. Mithredath was Cyrus's _____
5. "_____ of wickedness profit nothing"
6. Abraham's faith was "counted . . . to him for_____"
7. Another name for Ai
9. "Give _____"; to listen
10. Wood from which Noah built the ark
15. Another name for Noah
16. Egyptian god
19. Title for Egyptian ruler
22. Ezekiel said God would put _____ in Pharaoh's jaw
24. Sixteenth letter of the Greek alphabet
27. To humble
28. John saw that the New Jerusalem's gates will never be _____
29. "The sword to slay, and the dogs to _____"
30. Every Jewish _____ was circumcised
33. Malchus lost one temporarily
35. Indefinite article used 1,660 times in the Authorized Version

PUZZLE 94

1
2
3
4
5
6
7
8
9
10
11
12
13
14
15
16
17
18
19
20
21
22
23
24
25
26
27
28
29
30
31
32
33
34
35
36
37
38

ACROSS

1. He tried to become king instead of Solomon
4. "_____ not ye against the Lord"
6. Doeg the Edomite told Saul when David visited this town
9. Without yeast
11. "He smote them _____ and thigh"
12. She was a prostitute who became an ancestress of Jesus
14. "In the night _____ of Moab is laid waste"
15. Tamar's first husband
16. Once ruled by Melchizedek
17. Speed
19. One of Aram's sons
20. Moses' spokesman
21. Spear
24. David took Goliath's to Jerusalem
26. God will one day give the faithful a white _____ with a new name
28. "I am _____ of them that asked not for me"
30. Another word for stomach
32. "Amen" or "_____ be it"
33. Large assembly

DOWN

1. David's traitorous counselor
2. God is _____, everywhere at all times
3. One of Esau's three wives
5. Carried
7. God spoke to Moses from one
8. Mary was told that God's power would _____ her
10. Jesus' landing place after feeding the multitude
13. Old form of "to be"
18. "From _____ to _____, shall ye celebrate your sabbath"
22. Used in comparisons
23. Measure
25. Hanani the prophet rebuked this king
27. "Take thine _____, eat, drink, and be merry"
29. "What is a man profited, if he shall _____ the whole world, and lose his own soul?"
31. "_____ ye therefore, and teach all nations"

ACROSS

1. Branch of theology concerned with history's final events
7. Verb used to phrase a question
8. Can be an organ or a part of a plant
10. Another word for frost
11. Agur addressed his proverbs to him
13. One of David's mighty men; a Tizite
15. He bought his wife at a slave market after she left him
17. Midwife who saved Hebrew male children
19. Only water anyone walks on today
21. Abraham once camped between this city and Bethel
22. Act of God declaring men free of guilt
24. Turned to blood
25. Concubine of Esau's son Eliphaz
27. Metal mentioned five times in the Authorized Version
29. Abraham gave him tithes
33. Exclamation
35. God promised to "utterly put out the _____ of Amalek"

DOWN

2. Moses told God he was _____ of speech
3. "The Lord is . . . my buckler, and the _____ of my salvation"
4. One spelling of the last letter of the Hebrew alphabet
5. Adam and Eve sewed fig _____ together
6. "_____ must be born again"
7. Same as Iri
9. Commotion
12. Achan's father
13. Name of one of the two symbolic pillars in front of the temple
14. Direction referred to 2,484 times in the Authorized Version
16. Pertaining or belonging to; used 26,772 times in the Authorized Version
18. Called the most handsome man in Israel
20. City whose name meant "pasture"
21. Town near Pisidia where Paul and Barnabas preached on their first journey
22. Tree under which Elijah slept when fleeing from Jezebel
23. Could refer to physical blessings
26. What John did to a book at an angel's command
28. Isaiah mentioned this nation on the east side of the Tigris near Babylon
30. Bezalel's grandfather

PUZZLE 96

DOWN

31. Wilderness
32. "In the day that thou eatest thereof thou shalt surely _____"
34. Last Rephaite king of Bashan

ACROSS

1. Assyrian king; Sargon II's successor
8. Egyptian god
10. Moabite town or region
11. Abner's father
13. "Let God be true, but every man a _____"
14. King Jehoahaz died there
18. Ammonite god worshiped through child sacrifice
19. Egyptian god
20. Rehoboam's youngest son
22. Name meaning "God with us"
26. Probably another name for Jethro, Moses' father-in-law
27. Preposition used 2,696 times in the Authorized Version
28. Abram's Amorite ally
29. Personal pronoun used 4,402 times in the Authorized Version
31. One of five kings captured by Israel at the cave of Makkedah
32. Ruth was from there
33. Second city attacked by Israel in the Promised Land
35. "Man is not justified by the works of the _____"
37. Number of Fruit of the Spirit
38. Color of sky used to forecast weather
41. "That _____ serpent, called the Devil"
42. Exclamation used to get attention

DOWN

1. Murdered Sennacherib, his father
2. Its fuller name was No Amon, city of the god Amon
3. With his brother, he murdered Sennacherib his father
4. Egyptians were his principal descendants
5. Judah's wicked son
6. Preposition used 14,130 times in the Authorized Version
7. Daniel's Babylonian name included the name of this god
9. Paul started his journey to Rome on a ship from this port city
12. Paul told Titus that a church elder's children couldn't be accused of _____
15. Exclamation used only three times in the Authorized Version
16. One of five Midianite kings killed by Israel
17. Exclamation used 18 times in the Authorized Version
21. All family members and servants dwelling together
23. One of Ahasuerus's eunuchs
24. John the Baptist said he wasn't worthy to _____ Jesus' shoes
25. Two words; name of town where Mephibosheth lived before living with David
30. Preposition used 8,122 times in the Authorized Version; "For _____ us . . ."

DOWN

34. Town listed in Judah's inheritance in Joshua
36. Plural personal pronoun used 1,772 times in the Authorized Version
39. God

ACROSS

1. God said Cain would be "a _____ and a vagabond"
5. Name meaning "foolish"; he refused to help David
8. Personal singular pronoun used 4,402 times in the Authorized Version
9. Mizraim's son
10. Second baby born
12. Gomer's son
13. His bed was enormous
14. Indefinite pronoun used 6,875 times in the Authorized Version
15. Bethel's old name
17. Direction mentioned 1,121 times in the Authorized Version
18. "_____ eyed"; description of Leah
20. Early member of the tribe of Gad
21. Another Gadite who served David
22. Adonijah wanted to marry her; that cost him his life
25. Egyptian ruler
26. Agur addressed his proverbs to this person
27. Another word for "weak"
29. First son of Bilhah, Rachel's maid
31. Father of Phinehas and Hophni
32. Town situated at the head of the Gulf of Aqabah in Edom
33. He put away his foreign wife
34. Second son of Zilpah, Leah's maid

DOWN

1. One who helps in a task; Paul called Philemon this
2. He is Three in One
3. Jewish month between Sivan and Ab
4. "They gather the _____ of the wicked"; word used 10 times in the Authorized Version
5. Father of Jeroboam I
6. Healing ointment
7. "He made a decree for the rain, and a way for the _____"
8. Name given to the Wise Men
11. Judah's evil son
16. Member of a smaller family within the Kohathites of Levi
17. Waste product of refined metal
18. Letter introducing Psalm 119:169-176
19. On the high plain of Moab about 10 miles east of the Dead Sea
23. One of the chiefs under Nehemiah
24. Mountain in Galilee where the borders of Issachar, Zebulun, and Naphtali met
28. One of Ishmael's 12 sons
30. "The mouth of the foolish is _____ destruction"

PUZZLE 98

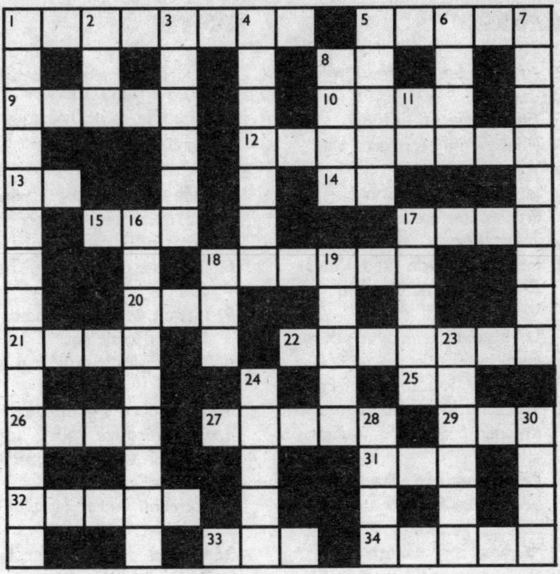

ACROSS

2. Area avoided by Jews in Jesus' day
7. City or region in Moab
8. Jeroboam II recovered this town for Israel
10. Jerahmeel's grandson
11. Preposition used 14,130 times in the Authorized Version
12. Indefinite article used 1,660 times in the Authorized Version
14. Love your _____ as yourself
16. Family
18. Annually floods part of Egypt
22. Musical instrument mentioned in Isaiah 5 and 14 and Amos 5 and 6
25. Peter preached, "Save yourselves from this _____ generation"
27. "A wise son maketh a _____ father"
29. Mountain opposite Mount Gerizim
32. Israelites were to _____ the Passover lamb
34. Jacob's action against Isaac
35. "The things which are seen are _____"
36. He ruled Egypt in Ahaz's day

DOWN

1. Agagite who tried to have the Jews slaughtered
3. "_____, and it shall be given you"
4. Jotham's son
5. Jude mentions those who "_____ greedily after the error of Balaam"
6. Surname of Lebbaeus the disciple
9. Nation which God used Gideon to defeat
10. Led an alliance of kings against Joshua
13. Zerubbabel's grandfather
15. Old word for "got"; used 20 times in the Authorized Version
17. Sixteenth letter of the Greek alphabet
19. Verb used 6,092 times in the Authorized Version
20. Site of famous Nabatean ruins east of the Jordan
21. Immoral, vulgar
23. Precious stone in third row on Aaron's breastplate
24. Twelfth letter of the Greek alphabet
26. "I will _____ in the house of the Lord for ever"
28. Zechariah 14 mentions this place
29. Action that brought earth's curse
30. To cut off; used only once in the Authorized Version
31. Measure
33. Number of people recorded who never saw death

PUZZLE 99

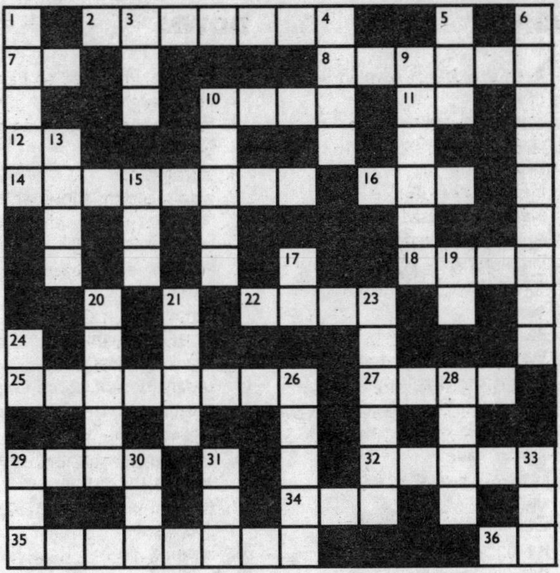

ACROSS

1. Saul tried to kill David with one twice
5. Servant of Solomon whose children returned from Babylon
8. Means "behold!"
10. Meditations; used once in the Authorized Version
13. Plural personal pronoun used 1,772 times in the Authorized Version
14. Beast of burden
15. What Samuel heard after Saul fought the Amalekites
18. Jews from Thessalonica turned the people of this town against Paul
19. Fifth letter of the Hebrew alphabet
21. Old word for "sinned"
24. Jair of Manasseh conquered this region under Moses
26. District governor who supplied Solomon with provisions from Benjamin
29. Indefinite article used 1,660 times in the Authorized Version
31. Act of consecration performed on Jewish males
34. Denotes exclusion from; used 684 times in the Authorized Version
36. Plural pronoun used 1,432 times in the Authorized Version
37. Water rose _____ cubits above the mountains during the Flood
38. One of the four rivers in Eden

DOWN

1. Eleventh
2. He raised Samuel
3. Haran's son
4. Negative
6. "In your _____ there remaineth falsehood"
7. People from a well-known city in Egypt
9. "As a _____ returneth to his vomit"
11. Found in Havilah
12. Hezekiah's mother
13. Exclamation of doom used 103 times in the Authorized Version
16. Old word for "know" used 10 times in the Authorized Version
17. God supplies them all
20. To sin
22. Kings reign, and _____ decree justice
23. "I delight to _____ thy will"
25. Zacharias's "lot was to _____ incense" when the angel appeared to him
27. Canaan's father
28. Captain of the guard who arrested Jeremiah
30. "Hear, ye _____; and look, ye blind"
32. "Whither I go, ye cannot _____"
33. Terah's family lived there
35. Conditional statement used 1,522 times in the Authorized Version

ACROSS

1. Meshezabeel's son who advised King Artaxerxes
5. Old word for "gladly"
9. One of five chief Philistine cities
11. Outcropping; word found only in the plural in I Kings 7 in the Authorized Version
12. "_____, a great multitude, which no man could number"
13. Another word for "hell"
15. To praise
17. To be somewhere; used 1,536 times in the Authorized Version
18. Preposition used 14,130 times in the Authorized Version
20. Satan is "the prince of the power of the _____"
22. Member of a family with the tribe of Reuben
25. Semiprecious material made by sea animals; mentioned in Job and Ezekiel
26. Equal to about 10 1/2 bushels by some estimates
27. Mountain where Balak took Balaam
28. Grain
30. Exclamation used 18 times in the Authorized Version
31. Landmark on the eastern border of the Promised Land
33. "_____ let not the Lord be angry"
34. Negative response
35. What Jesus called Jairus's daughter

DOWN

1. One of the places Paul visited
2. Rabbi
3. He stole loot from Jericho and brought defeat from Ai
4. One who worships an image
6. Jewish believer once imprisoned with Paul
7. He built an ark
8. Rahab hid the spies under it
10. Verb used 1,331 times in the Authorized Version
14. Terah's father
15. "Those that seek me _____ shall find me"
16. "The brass, the iron, the _____"
19. Father of Asaph the singer
21. Indefinite article used 6,875 times in the Authorized Version
23. Sons of Zerah
24. Can indicate direction
25. Part of the booty taken by Gideon
27. Ezekiel used an iron one
29. Nehemiah's coworker
31. Father of a giant race
32. Maiden Greek mythology
35. Giant mentioned in 2 Samuel had twelve of this digit
36. "Eyes have they, but they _____ not"

PUZZLE 101

ACROSS

37. Indicates a choice; used 1,015 times in the Authorized Version
38. Another name for En-mishpat
39. Manasseh's grandson through Machir

SOLUTIONS

Puzzle 1, Page 7

Puzzle 2, Page 9

Puzzle 3, Page 11

Puzzle 4, Page 13

Puzzle 5, Page 15

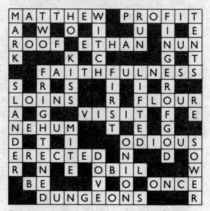

Puzzle 6, Page 17

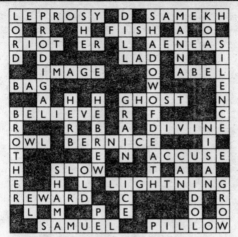

Puzzle 7, Page 19

Puzzle 8, Page 21

Puzzle 9, Page 23

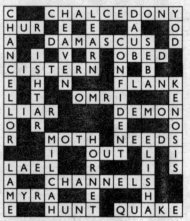

Puzzle 10, Page 25

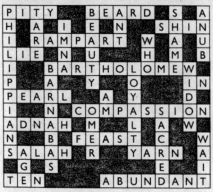

Puzzle 11, Page 27

Puzzle 12, Page 29

Puzzle 13, Page 31

Puzzle 14, Page 33

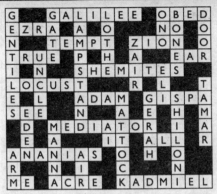

Puzzle 15, Page 35

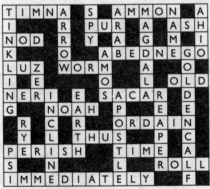

Puzzle 16, Page 37

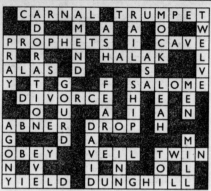

Puzzle 17, Page 39

Puzzle 18, Page 41

Puzzle 19, Page 43

Puzzle 20, Page 45

Puzzle 21, Page 47

Puzzle 22, Page 49

Puzzle 23, Page 51

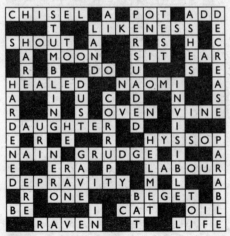

Puzzle 24, Page 53

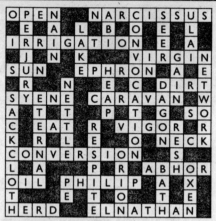

Puzzle 25, Page 55

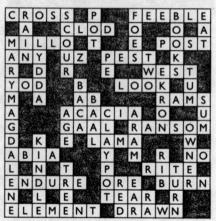

Puzzle 26, Page 57

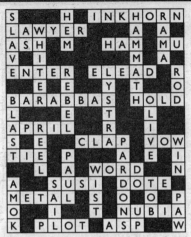

Puzzle 27, Page 59

Puzzle 28, Page 61

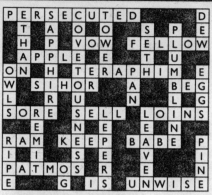

Puzzle 29, Page 63

Puzzle 30, Page 65

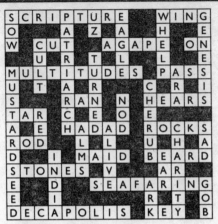

Puzzle 31, Page 67

Puzzle 32, Page 69

Puzzle 33, Page 71

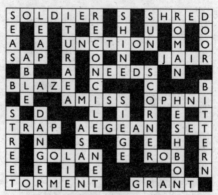

Puzzle 34, Page 73

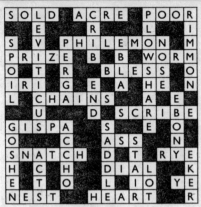

Puzzle 35, Page 75

Puzzle 36, Page 77

227

Puzzle 37, Page 79

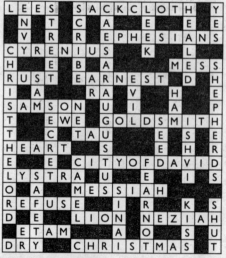

Puzzle 38, Page 81

Puzzle 39, Page 83

Puzzle 40, Page 85

Puzzle 41, Page 87

Puzzle 42, Page 89

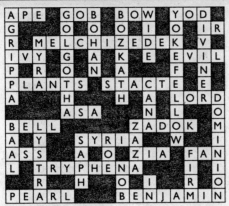

Puzzle 43, Page 91

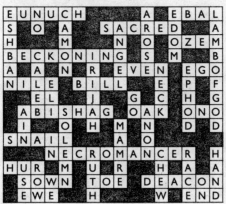

Puzzle 44, Page 93

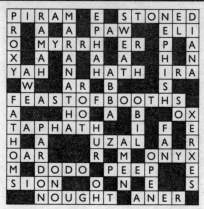

Puzzle 45, Page 95

Puzzle 46, Page 97

Puzzle 47, Page 99

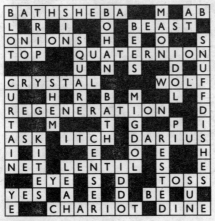

Puzzle 48, Page 101

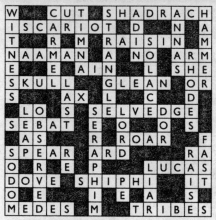

Puzzle 49, Page 103

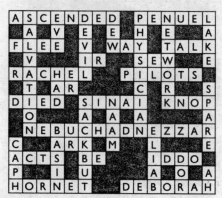

Puzzle 50, Page 105

234

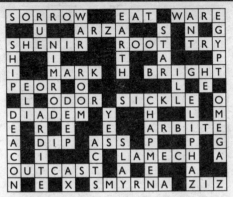

Puzzle 51, Page 107

Puzzle 52, Page 109

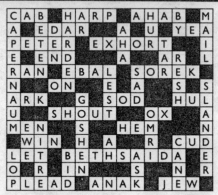

Puzzle 53, Page 111

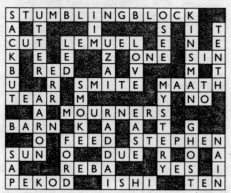

Puzzle 54, Page 113

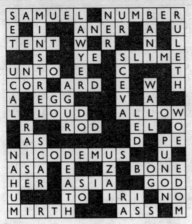

Puzzle 55, Page 115

Puzzle 56, Page 117

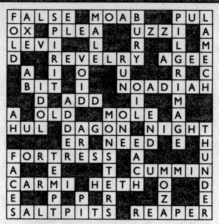

Puzzle 57, Page 119

Puzzle 58, Page 121

Puzzle 59, Page 123

Puzzle 60, Page 125

Puzzle 61, Page 127

Puzzle 62, Page 129

Puzzle 63, Page 131

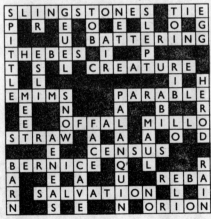

Puzzle 64, Page 133

241

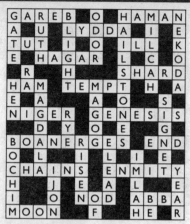

Puzzle 65, Page 135

Puzzle 66, Page 137

Puzzle 67, Page 139

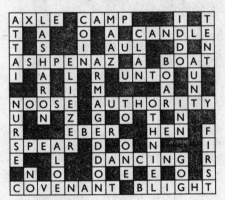

Puzzle 68, Page 141

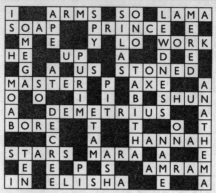

Puzzle 69, Page 143

Puzzle 70, Page 145

Puzzle 71, Page 147

Puzzle 72, Page 149

Puzzle 73, Page 151

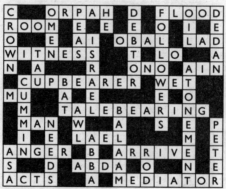

Puzzle 74, Page 153

Puzzle 75, Page 155

Puzzle 76, Page 157

Puzzle 77, Page 159

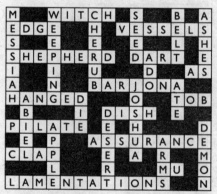

Puzzle 78, Page 161

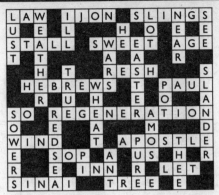

Puzzle 79, Page 163

Puzzle 80, Page 165

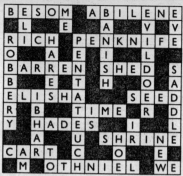

Puzzle 81, Page 167

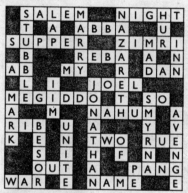

Puzzle 82, Page 169

Puzzle 83, Page 171

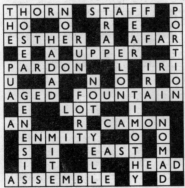

Puzzle 84, Page 173

Puzzle 85, Page 175

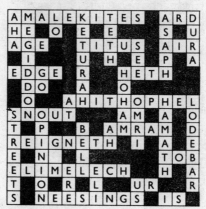

Puzzle 86, Page 177

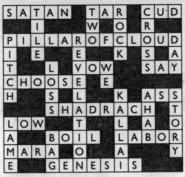

Puzzle 87, Page 179

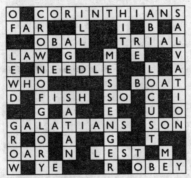

Puzzle 88, Page 181

253

Puzzle 89, Page 183

Puzzle 90, Page 185

254

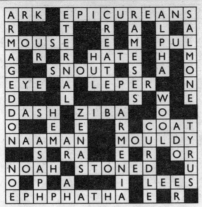

Puzzle 91, Page 187

Puzzle 92, Page 189

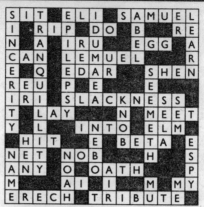

Puzzle 93, Page 191

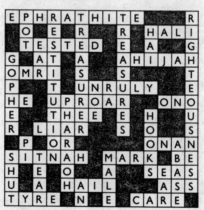

Puzzle 94, Page 193

Puzzle 95, Page 195

Puzzle 96, Page 197

Puzzle 97, Page 199

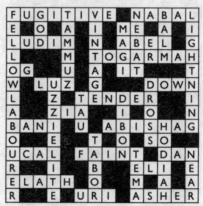

Puzzle 98, Page 201

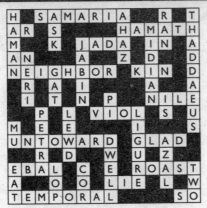

Puzzle 99, Page 203

Puzzle 100, Page 205

Puzzle 101, Page 207

Other Living Books Best-Sellers

ANSWERS by Josh McDowell and Don Stewart. In a question-and-answer format, the authors tackle sixty-five of the most-asked questions about the Bible, God, Jesus Christ, miracles, other religions, and creation. 07-0021-X

THE BEST OF BIBLE TRIVIA I: KINGS, CRIMINALS, SAINTS, AND SINNERS by J. Stephen Lang. A fascinating book containing over 1,500 questions and answers about the Bible arranged topically in over 50 categories. Taken from the best-selling **Complete Book of Bible Trivia.** 07-0464-9

THE CHILD WITHIN by Mari Hanes. The author shares insights she gained from God's Word during her own pregnancy. She identifies areas of stress, offers concrete data about the birth process, and points to God's sure promises that he will gently lead those that are with young. 07-0219-0

CHRISTIANITY: THE FAITH THAT MAKES SENSE by Dennis McCallum. New and inquiring Christians will find spiritual support in this readable apologetic, which presents a clear, rational defense for Christianity to those unfamiliar with the Bible. 07-0525-4

COME BEFORE WINTER AND SHARE MY HOPE by Charles R. Swindoll. A collection of brief vignettes offering hope and the assurance that adversity and despair are temporary setbacks we can overcome! 07-0477-0

THE COMPLETE GUIDE TO BIBLE VERSIONS by Philip W. Comfort. A guidebook with descriptions of all the English translations and suggestions for their use. Includes the history of biblical writings. 07-1251-X

DARE TO DISCIPLINE by James Dobson. A straightforward, plainly written discussion about building and maintaining parent/child relationships based upon love, respect, authority, and ultimate loyalty to God. 07-0522-X

DR. DOBSON ANSWERS YOUR QUESTIONS by James Dobson. In this convenient reference book, renowned author Dr. James Dobson addresses heartfelt concerns on many topics, including marital relationships, infant care, child discipline, home management, and others. 07-0580-7

Other Living Books Best-Sellers

JOHN, SON OF THUNDER by Ellen Gunderson Traylor. In this saga of adventure, romance, and discovery, travel with John—the disciple whom Jesus loved—down desert paths, through the courts of the Holy City, and to the foot of the cross as he leaves his luxury as a privileged son of Israel for the bitter hardship of his exile on Patmos. 07-1903-4

LIFE IS TREMENDOUS! by Charlie "Tremendous" Jones. Believing that enthusiasm makes the difference, Jones shows how anyone can be happy, involved, relevant, productive, healthy, and secure in the midst of a high-pressure, commercialized society. 07-2184-5

LORD, COULD YOU HURRY A LITTLE? by Ruth Harms Calkin. These prayer-poems from the heart of a godly woman trace the inner workings of the heart, following the rhythms of the day and seasons of the year with expectation and love. 07-3816-0

LORD, I KEEP RUNNING BACK TO YOU by Ruth Harms Calkin. In prayer-poems tinged with wonder, joy, humanness, and questioning, the author speaks for all of us who are groping and learning together what it means to be God's child. 07-3819-5

MORE THAN A CARPENTER by Josh McDowell. A hard-hitting book for people who are skeptical about Jesus' deity, his resurrection, and his claim on their lives. 07-4552-3

MOUNTAINS OF SPICES by Hannah Hurnard. Here is an allegory comparing the nine spices mentioned in the Song of Solomon to the nine fruits of the Spirit. A story of the glory of surrender by the author of **Hinds' Feet on High Places.** 07-4611-2

QUICK TO LISTEN, SLOW TO SPEAK by Robert E. Fisher. Families are shown how to express love to one another by developing better listening skills, finding ways to disagree without arguing, and using constructive criticism. 07-5111-6

RAINBOW COTTAGE by Grace Livingston Hill. Safe at last, Sheila tries to forget the horrors of the past, unaware that terror is about to close in on her again. 07-5731-9

Other Living Books Best-Sellers

THE SECRET OF LOVING by Josh McDowell. McDowell explores the values and qualities that will help both the single and married reader to be the right person for someone else. 07-5845-5

SUCCESS: THE GLENN BLAND METHOD by Glenn Bland. The author shows how to set goals and make plans that really work. His ingredients for success include spiritual, financial, educational, and recreational balances. 07-6689-X

WHAT WIVES WISH THEIR HUSBANDS KNEW ABOUT WOMEN by James Dobson. The best-selling author of **Dare to Discipline** and **The Strong-Willed Child** brings us this vital book that speaks to the unique emotional needs and aspirations of today's woman. An immensely practical, interesting guide. 07-7896-0

WINDOW TO MY HEART by Joy Hawkins. A collection of heartfelt poems aptly expressing common emotions and thoughts that single women of any age experience. The author's vital trust in a loving God is evident throughout. 07-7977-0

If you are unable to find any of these titles at your local bookstore, you may call Tyndale's toll-free number **1-800-323-9400, X-214** for ordering information. Or you may write for pricing to **Tyndale Family Products, P.O. Box 448, Wheaton, IL 60189-0448**.